- Note from the Publisher -

Welcome to a glimpse into the world of international quilting. At Stitch Publications our wish is for you to be able to explore beyond the boundaries of the country you live in to experience and see what other fiber artists are doing.

In many countries, rather than learning from various books, quilters study under a single master, spending years progressing from simple techniques to the extremely difficult. Intricate designs are celebrated and sewing and quilting by hand is honored and as such, hand-quilting is the typical method used to quilt.

This book was written in its original language, Japanese, by a master quilter, Yoko Saito. We have done our best to make the directions for each project easy to understand if you have some level of quilting experience, while maintaining the appearance and intent of the original author and publisher.

We hope the beautifully designed handmade items in this book inspire and encourage you to make them for yourself.

- Important Tips Before You Begin -

These facts might suggest that intermediate or advanced quilters will be more comfortable working on these projects.

- Techniques -

Certain detailed descriptions of specific techniques in earlier projects are not repeated in later projects. It is advisable to read through the book from the beginning, even if making a project that appears later in the book, as earlier projects may describe key techniques in detail.

- Measurements -

The original designs were created using the metric system for dimensions. In order to assist you, we have included the imperial system measurements in brackets. However, please note that samples that appear in the book were created and tested using the metric system. Thus, you will find that if you use the imperial measurements to make the projects, the items you make will not be exactly the same size as when using the metric measurements. Please also note that seam allowances are called out in separately and highlighted in boxes.

- Patterns/Templates -

Patterns for each project appear in several different ways: a) as dimensional diagrams b) in the pattern sheet inserts c) in the body of the text d) illustrations. One must read through all the instructions carefully to understand what size to cut the fabric and related materials including instructions for each project relating to seam allowances.

Stitch Publications, 2012

Yoko Saito's
houses, houses, houses

Foreword

The first house quilt block that I remember seeing was that of the classic "schoolhouse." It was a very simple pattern with a triangle for the roof and rectangles that made up the chimney, windows and doors. I fell in love with it immediately as I imagined a mother who lovingly sends her happy and energetic children off to school.

The wonderful thing about pieced blocks and appliqués of houses are that anyone can easily create one of their own. Even if you start with the same basic house pattern, just by changing the fabric used for the walls or roof will make it completely unique. You can get creative and think about changing the shape of a door, or making it appear that there is a light shining out of a window. You can even add trees outside the house. It is almost as though you are young again and playing with blocks, putting them together however you desire.

Ideas for house blocks can come from anywhere. You might stop and sketch a building that you see on a corner when you are out walking, find one in a picture book, or be inspired by a photo you took while on holiday.

In this book you will find many projects with varying interpretations of houses from one-dimensional, to silhouettes, as well as the cutest mini-quilted houses. I hope that this book sparks your imagination and encourages you to create your own original house.

Yoko Saito

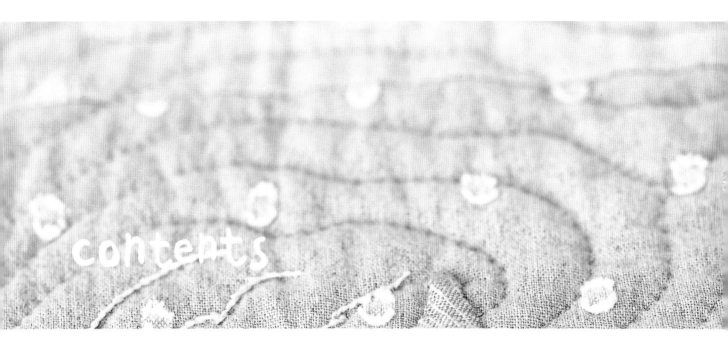

contents

going out with my house

a house surrounded by trees

stairs

storehouses in the dark

a general store

an apartment building

a dog at work; a cat at play

on my way home

going uphill, 'round and 'round

antennas

the view of a chimney sweep

japanese houses

windmills

going out with my house

a house surrounded by trees

A small cottage peeps out between the trees like in a fairytale.
How enchanting it would be if you came upon this house while out for a walk.
A simple symmetrical design makes this pleasing to the eye.

 →page 67

Placing the staircase with a different visual perspective to the background and making the balustrade a focal point gives a modern setting to the bag.

→page 60

storehouses in the dark

The dark night sky; only the silhouettes of warehouses
emerge, creating a fantastic repeated pattern.

a general store

I imagined Mr. Oleson's shop from "Little House
on the Prairie" when I designed this bag. Any
moment I expect Laura to open the door.

an apartment building

Apartments within this cute house-shaped coin purse are small, but comfortable. Designed with a side zipper, it is easy to use.

a dog at work; a cat at play

The guard dog awaits the return of its master. The fence becomes part of the design. This is a perfect water bottle holder.

→page 85・86

on my way home

The night rain lightly falls as I rush home.
Through the trees, the lights of the
house come into view. Soon it will be
time for dinner.

 →page 87

going uphill, 'round and 'round

Looking out of the window of the train, I see the landscape
go by. Images of houses from books and wrapping paper;
buildings I see when I walk our dog in the neighborhood
flit through my mind.

➔page 88

antennas

As night begins to fall, I see lights come on, one by one, in the windows of the houses. The antennas on the roofs stand out against the dark sky.

the view of a chimney sweep

I envisioned the rooftops from the movie, "Mary Poppins", where the chimney sweeps spontaneously danced under the stars.

→page 89

japanese houses

A picture in a travel magazine reveals an old cobblestone street lined with Japanese "sake" warehouses. The fabric chosen for the bag harmonizes with the overall concept and design.

windmills

The blades of the windmills in the shape of
a cross stand out impressively in this design.
Contrasting texture and color peek out through
the gusset.

→page 93

little houses in my bag

linus's little red house

birdhouses

a bike parked on a corner

loft windows

i'm home!

in the woods

flying high in the sky

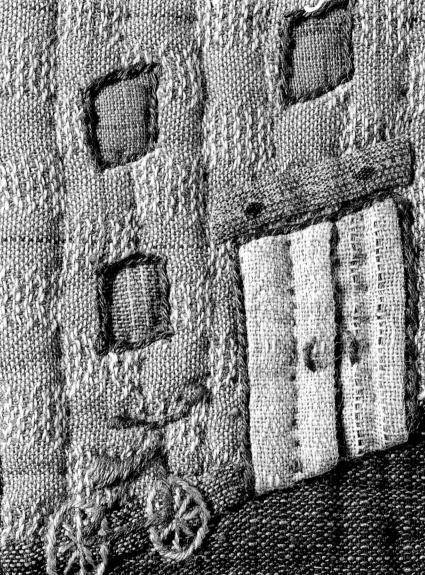

little houses in my bag

linus's little red house

This little pouch shows a miniature of the little doghouse that our own dog, Linus, was fond of. The acorn zipper pull coordinates with the acorn-inspired background fabric.

birdhouses

I love birdhouses. Although I don't have a garden
myself, I tend to want to display them within my home.
Can you hear the chirping of the birds?

→page 95

a bike parked on a corner

A bike parked in a quiet back alley between buildings
made the perfect design for this little coin purse.

→page 96

loft windows

The flap of this little bag showcases windows in the loft, while the door, when slipped through the flap, doubles as the fastener.

→page 97

i'm home!

With the gate partially open, it appears as though someone just came home. The zipper disappears perfectly into the roofline of this cute little pencil case.

→page 98

in the woods

A little house nestled in a forest of trees is the focus in this small roly-poly bag.

 →page 99

flying high in the sky

In one of my favorite movies there is a scene in which a grandmother, who sells bird seed, watches a flock of doves fly off into the sunset sky.

→page 100

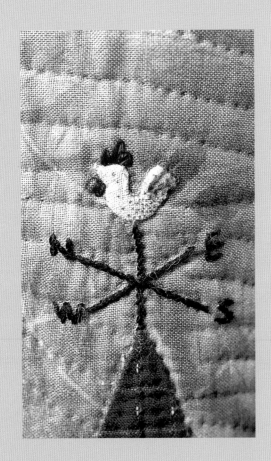

my life with my beloved houses

falling snow

a holiday cottage

an autumn breeze

houses in a foreign country

my hometown

a town on a hill

house-shaped blocks

an old castle

buildings

my life with my beloved houses

falling snow

The quilting in the background gives the illusion of falling snow in this placemat design.

→page 101

a holiday cottage

Made with heavily-quilted fabric, this tea cozy is designed in the shape of a little cottage with a chimney and sloping roof.

→page 102

an autumn breeze

The brisk autumn breeze blows between the houses and can be seen in the background quilting.

→page 101

houses in a foreign country

The cushions are designed to look like exotic little palaces
that are adorned with pom-poms and pieced with wool...so
warm to the touch.

→page 103

my hometown

Using the skyline of the town as part of the design creates interest. A perfect decorative accent for a shelf, or to use as a letter holder.

a town on a hill

Designing the appliquéd sides of this carry-all with densely packed houses gives a sense of artistic perspective.

→page 105

house-shaped blocks

These soft little blocks in the shape of houses make you want to pick them up and play with them. They are cute, lined up side by side.

→page 106

an old castle

The turrets of the castle look like little hats with the flags streaming in the wind. Use it as a handbag or a catch-all.

 →page 108

buildings

In memory of my trip to New York City , this
design shows the top of the skyline in the city.
A perfect tissue box holder.

→page 110

let's build a town with my houses!

walking about town

block of the month I

block of the month II

on a street corner

the chatter of houses

your favorite house

walking about town

Perfect for hallways or wall areas that need a narrow wall quilt. Even while you are in your house, it is as though you are walking about town.

→page 51

block of the month I

Two houses are in each month's design. Working steadily,
your town will be finished within a year.

→page 70

block of the month II

An extra row of houses were added to the Block of the Month I for this quilt.
Feel free to change the width and length and create your own town.

on a street corner

A variation of the block of the month quilt, houses in the
border create a cheerful appearance.

 →page 79

the chatter of houses

Houses chitchat with each other in the night while the snow lightly falls. This
is a fun quilt for beginners since the houses are all created free form.

→page 80

your favorite house

Why not create memories of your own trips in quilts? I
designed these patterns from photographs that I had taken
when we visited the Alsace region in autumn.

Alsatian House III

Before you begin...

- All measurements listed for the following projects are in centimeters (cm) and inches [in brackets].
- The dimensions of the finished project are listed for each, as well as shown in the drawings. Note that the quilted pieces tend to shrink somewhat depending on the type of fabric used, the thickness of the batting, the amount of quilting and individual quilting technique.
- Typically, both the sewing and quilting thread should be the same color as the fabric you are working with. However, use a beige-colored thread if you wish the quilting to stand out.
- Seam allowances will be specified for each project. However, in general, add 0.3-0.5 cm [⅛"~¼"] for appliqué pieces, 0.7 cm [¼"] for piecing, and a generous 3-5 cm [1¼"~2"] for backing, considering shrinkage due to quilting and binding.
- Please see p. 65 for basic terms used in quilting.

Step by step

There are many traditional house patterns available in the market, and many of them are appealing. But wouldn't it be wonderful if you could make your own house pattern? Use these "step by step" directions to make your own house.

If you are new to drafting your own patterns from photos, stick to less complicated designs.

1. Decide the finished size of the house you want to make and whether the house will be two or three-dimensional. For a two-dimensional house, draw a line straight across for its bottom. Decide on a focal point in the photo and begin drawing from there. With the photo above, the focal point is the small dormer window. Next, draw the rooflines, sides of the house, windows and doors. Draw a rough design first before you refine it.

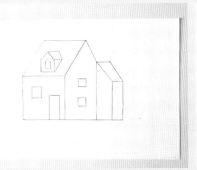

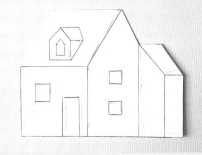

2. Now re-draw your rough draft into a well-proportioned and neat drawing (using graph paper often helps). This is the design that you will use as your template. Using the template, or making a copy, cut out each piece of the template and label if necessary.

3. Now comes the fun part of choosing your fabrics. First, decide on the background fabric. Be creative as to the time of day: black for night, grey for a cloudy day or a snow-like pattern for a snowy day. While looking at the photo, choose your fabrics for the walls, roof and other key sections by arranging them on the background fabric until you get the combination you like. It is best to pick contrasting or accent colors for windows and doors.

4. Using the individual pieces of the template, cut out the fabric pieces; add appropriate seam allowances to each piece before you cut. Place the pieces on the background before sewing to see if you like your choices. Now is the time to change anything you don't like. Piece or appliqué your house together.

Variations

Alsatian House I

Look for fabric that has the look of brick walls, window grids and stained windows. Add embroidery to create the details on the clock, windows and other areas to which you want to add embellishments.

Alsatian House II

Embroidery embellishment is a great way to add design elements to any house. This looks particularly wonderful when you add flower boxes to the windows using stitches that are pronounced. Add all the elements that you see in the photo as you like.

Alsatian House III

It is also easy to combine piecing and appliqué to your design. Appliqué the roof of the tower, the nest and birds on top of the pieced buildings.

Essential Quilting Notions & Tools

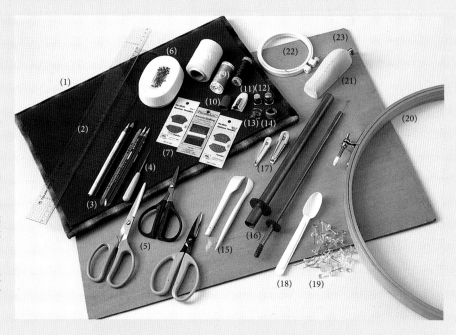

(1) Non-Slip Board
The non-slip surface side of the board is used when marking fabric or when using the fabric pressing tools to turn under the seam allowances. The soft side backed with batting and fabric can be used as a mini ironing surface.

(2) Rulers
Used to trace straight lines when transferring patterns. Rulers with markings made for quilters are useful.

(3) Pencils • Colored Pencils • Chalk Pencils
[Pencils] Used for copying patterns, or marking quilting lines. If you use a pencil to mark quilting lines, use one with soft lead. [Colored Pencils] Used for marking the wrong side of fabric. The lines won't always disappear, so do not use for marking quilting lines.
[Chalk Pencils] Used to make marks on fabric where pencil lines won't show up well.

(4) Awl
To mark points when transferring and drawing patterns.

(5) Scissors
They will last longer if used for specific things, such as for paper, fabric or thread.

(6) Straight Pins • Magnetic Pin Cushion
[Straight Pins] It is easiest to use ones that are very fine and have small heads.
[Magnetic Pin Cushion] Using a magnetic pin cushion takes less effort than traditional ones.

(7) Appliqué Needles • Quilting Betweens Needles • Basting Needles
[Appliqué Needles] A long, thin needle approximately 3 cm [1¼"] long, used for piecing and appliqué.
[Quilting Betweens Needles] A short needle approximately 2.5 cm [1"] long used specifically for quilting.
[Basting Needles] A long needle used for basting.

(8) Basting Thread
Used for basting.

(9) Quilting Thread • Sewing Thread
[Quilting Thread] A coated, durable thread used for hand-quilting. [Sewing Thread] Used for piecing or stitching; appropriate for either hand-sewing or machine sewing.

(10) Rubber Finger Tips
Wear on your right index finger during quilting or appliqué to help grab the needle and reduce slippage.

(11) Leather Thimble
Slip this over a metal thimble on your middle finger as you work to keep work from slipping.

(12) Metal Thimble
Used to push the needle through cloth when quilting. (Flat and Round Head)

(13) Ring Cutter
Conveniently worn on your left (or right) thumb and used for cutting threads as you are working.

(14) Adjustable Thimble
Used when piecing by hand.

(15) Seam Pressing Tools
Use to press seam allowance down in lieu of ironing when working with appliqué pieces. (Finger Presser, Hera Markers). See p. 53 for their use.

(16) Tube Turners
Used to turn fabric tubes right side out or for making piping cord.

(17) Bias Tape Maker
Used to guide bias strips through as you iron to make binding.

(18) Spoon
Often used when pin-basting a quilt. Safety pins are easy to use for this method.

(19) Push Pins
Useful to keep layers from shifting when getting ready to baste quilt sandwich. The longer the pin, the better.

(20) Quilting Hoop
Used to hold the quilt sandwich during quilting. It can also be used as a makeshift light table by holding it up to a window to transfer a pattern onto the fabric.

(21) Weights (paperweights, beanbags, etc.)
Used to weigh down a small quilt when quilting.

(22) Embroidery Hoop
To hold fabric while doing fine embroidery stitches.

(23) Basting Board
Any smooth wooden board used for basting small projects in lieu of a tabletop.

*Other notions and tools such as glue sticks and curved needles will be called for as well.

* Contrasting thread has been used in the photos for instructional purposes.

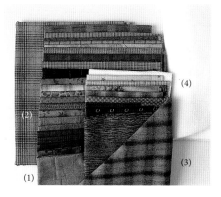

Wall Quilt: **Walking About Town** Shown on p. 40

• The full-size template/pattern can be found on Side A of the pattern sheet inserts.
• Finished measurement: 29.4 × 121.4 cm [11⅝" × 47⅞"]

Materials Needed

(1) Cottons
Assorted fat quarters or scraps (piecing and appliqué)
Brown print - 7 × 122 cm [2¾" × 48"] (street)
Beige homespun (5 different) - 28 × 26 cm each [11" × 10¼"] (background)
(2) Homespun - 40 × 130 cm [15¾" × 51⅛"] (backing)
(3) Homespun - 3.5 × 310 cm [1⅜" × 118"] (binding)
(4) Batting - 40 × 130 cm [15¾" × 51⅛"]
Embroidery thread - lt beige, beige, brown, dk brown, grey, bordeaux, black, 3 shades of green

Seam allowances: add 0.3-0.5 cm [⅛"~¼"] to appliqué; 0.7 cm [¼"] to piecing; prepare the backing and batting by cutting them to 40 × 130 cm [15¼" × 51⅛"]

Dimensional Diagram

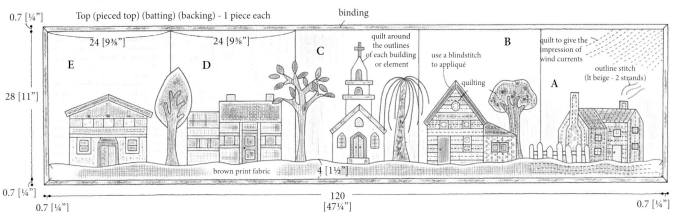

0.7 [¼"]

Top (pieced top) (batting) (backing) - 1 piece each

binding

24 [9⅜"]   24 [9⅜"]

C

quilt around the outlines of each building or element

B

quilt to give the impression of wind currents

use a blindstitch to appliqué

outline stitch (lt beige - 2 strands)

E   D   quilting   A

28 [11"]

brown print fabric   4 [1½"]

0.7 [¼"]

0.7 [¼"]   120 [47¼"]   0.7 [¼"]

1. Making templates.

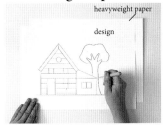

heavyweight paper

design

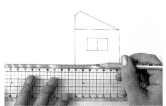

1. Using the pattern, either trace it onto heavyweight paper or make a photocopy. Place the design on top of the paper and use the awl to mark the corners of each specific pattern piece.

2. Use a ruler to connect the dots made by the awl in step 1 on the heavyweight paper.

3. Use a glue stick to tack the design in step 1 onto another sheet of heavyweight paper. Cut out each pattern piece. (You might need to make several in order to get all of the individual pieces.)

* Follow instructions in step 3 to make templates for designs with curved lines as they will be difficult to draw with a ruler. You will only need one each of any specific size or pattern.

2. Cutting out the fabric pieces.

  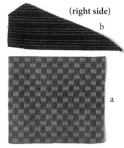

(right side)

b

b (wrong side)

a

1. With the wrong side up, lay the fabric on the non-slip surface side of the board. Place the template 0.7 cm [¼"] from the outside edge of the fabric and use a marking pencil to trace the finished sewing line of the template.

2. Repeat for each template piece, matching the template piece to the pattern of the fabric that you want to use.

3. Make sure to add 0.7 cm [¼"] seam allowance to each piece before cutting.

3. Sewing your house design together.

Directions - House B

1. Piecing

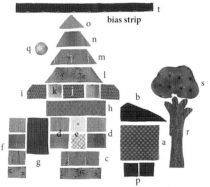  

1. Cut patterns for piecing, "a" to "p" with a 0.7 cm [¼"] seam allowance and the appliqué pieces, "q" to "s" with a 0.3-0.5 cm [⅛"~¼"] seam allowance. Prepare a 2 cm [¾"] wide bias strip (measure the roofline - p. 54 - for length).

2. For the first section, with right sides together, pin pieces "a" and "b" matching corners and edges.

3. Knot the thread and take one stitch at the marked dot at the corner. Insert the needle into the same place again and take another stitch (single backstitch).

4. Sew along the finished sewing line to the opposite corner using a running stitch. Gently pull the fabric with your thumb and index finger, making sure that the fabric is lying flat and the stitches aren't pulling.

5. Finish with a backstitch at the marked dot at the corner and knot the thread.

6. Trim the seam allowance down to 0.7 cm [¼"].

7. Fold the finished seam toward piece "b" and finger press, leaving 0.1 cm [¹/₁₆"] showing over the fold to hide the seam.

8. Open up the piecing and press flat.

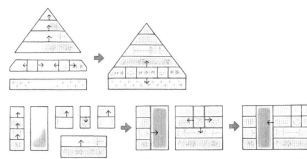

blindstitch

sew

9. Sew the two window pieces "p" together down the center as shown; press the seams to one side. Using one of the pressing tools, crease along the finished sewing lines. Place the window unit on piece "a" (as shown above) and using a blindstitch, appliqué it onto the side of the house. This completes segment 1.

10. For segment 2, sew the smaller pieces together in the same manner as the directions on p. 52. Appliqué the small round window "q" onto the block.

2. Appliqué * Place the appliqués wherever you desire on the background fabric.

leave open

1. Use a marking pencil to trace the location of the appliqué onto the background fabric (cut to 26 × 25.5 cm [10¼" × 10"]). Position and pin pattern piece "s" in place. Using a blindstitch, sew the appliqué in place, turning the edges under with the tip of the needle as you sew. Clip the seam allowances in the curves to help with ease.

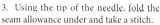

blindstitch

2. Next, position and pin pattern piece "r" in place on the outline. Beginning on the right side of tree trunk, blindstitch to just before the tip of the first limb. Snip off the rabbit ear.
3. Using the tip of the needle, fold the seam allowance under and take a stitch.
4. Repeat to get a neat corner and continue to sew to the inner curve.

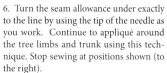

5. Clip the seam allowance in the inner curve, being careful not to go beyond the marked sewing line.

6. Turn the seam allowance under exactly to the line by using the tip of the needle as you work. Continue to appliqué around the tree limbs and trunk using this technique. Stop sewing at positions shown (to the right).

8. Using a seam pressing tool, make creases along the finished sewing line as shown. Then fold the seam allowances in along the creases and press again from the right side.

leave open

(wrong side)

(wrong side)

7. As part of the design will overlap this area (shown above), do not stitch the bottom of the tree trunk and left side.

10. With the seam allowances pressed under, place segment 2 in position so that it slightly overlaps segment 1. Pin in place and appliqué onto the background, leaving the bottom and the roofline open.

9. Position and pin segment 1 (from step 8) on the background fabric and using a blindstitch, sew up the right side and roof. Leave the bottom open where there will be overlap.

0.9 [½"]

12. Leaving an extra 0.5 cm [½"] free at one end, position the bias tape along the roofline, folding the tape at the top of the roof at an angle. Pin in place. Leaving 0.5 cm [½"] at the end, trim off any excess. Baste in place.

11. Using the bias strip "t" and referring to p. 81, create bias tape that is 0.9 cm [½"] wide.

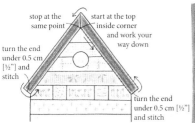

stop at the same point

start at the top inside corner and work your way down

turn the end under 0.5 cm [½"] and stitch

turn the end under 0.5 cm [½"] and stitch

Directions - House A

1. Cut patterns for piecing, "a" to "f" with a 0.7 cm [¼"] seam allowance and the appliqué pieces, "g" to "k" with a 0.3-0.5 cm [⅛"~¼"] seam allowance.

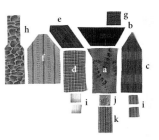

13. Refer to the diagram above and using a blindstitch, sew the roof in place. This completes the block for House B.

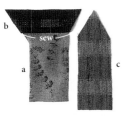

b

sew

a

c

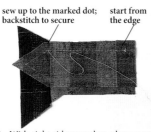

sew up to the marked dot; backstitch to secure

start from the edge

start from the marked dot

backstitch at the marked dot

2. To create segment 1, and following the directions from House B, sew pattern pieces "a" and "b" together. Press seam allowance toward piece "b".

3. With right sides together, place pattern piece "c" on top of the piece just made, as shown, and sew from the edge to the marked dot. Backstitch at the corner dot to secure, manipulate the pieces to match the roofline; pin. Continue to sew up the side of the roofline to the marked dot; backstitch. Press seam allowance toward piece "a".

4. To create segment 2, with right sides together, sew pattern pieces "d" and "e" together. Press the seam allowance toward piece "e". Next, sew "d" and "f" together as you did for segment 1. Press the seam allowance to one side.

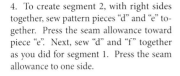

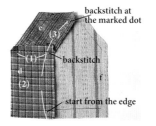

backstitch at the marked dot

backstitch

start from the edge

backstitch

backstitch

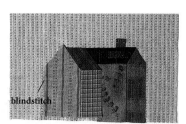

5. Use a marking pencil to trace the location of the appliqué onto the background fabric. For pattern piece "g", turn the seam allowance under on three sides and sew it onto the background fabric (leave the bottom open.) Then position segment 1; pin and blindstitch in place.

6. Press seam allowance on segment 2 (except for the bottom). Position and pin in place, overlapping segment 1; blindstitch to the background.

7. Press seam allowances under for pattern piece "h" (except for the bottom). Position and pin in place as shown; blindstitch.

8. Appliqué the door and windows. use a marking pencil to draw smoke coming out of the chimney. Embroider the smoke onto the background. using two strands of beige thread and an outline stitch. This completes the block for House A.

Directions - House C

1. Cut patterns for piecing, "c", "h" and "j" with a 0.7 cm [¼"] seam allowance; the 1.3 cm [½"] bias strip and appliqué pieces, with a 0.3-0.5 cm [⅛"~¼"] seam allowance.

With a marking pencil, draw the appliqué design on the right sides of pattern pieces "c", "e" and "j".

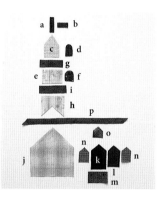

2. With right sides together, position and pin pattern piece "a"; blindstitch between dots.

3. Flip piece "a" over and finger press. Fold under the seam allowance at the top just to the marked sewing line. Blindstitch in place.

4. Use the tip of the needle to turn the seam allowance under and continue to blindstitch to the background, making sure to stitch neat corners. Leave the bottom open.

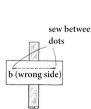
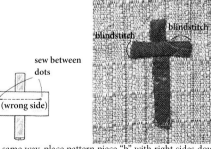

5. In the same way, place pattern piece "b" with right sides down, aligning to the finished sewing line. Pin and blindstitch between dots. Flip piece "b" over and finger press. Use the tip of the needle to turn the seam allowance under as you go (see diagram above left).

6. Sew pattern piece "c" in place and appliqué pattern piece "d" on top. Do not sew the bottom of "c" and "d".

7. For pattern piece "e", turn seam allowance under and blindstitch the left and right sides. Appliqué piece "f" on top.

8. Fold the seam allowances under for pattern piece "g". Position and pin in place; blindstitch on top of both pieces, covering raw edges.

baste in place

9. Position in place and pin pattern piece "h" to the background; blindstitch on the left and right sides. Sew pattern piece "i" in place using the same technique as on p. 55. Place pattern piece "j" on top and blindstitch the left and right sides. Sew on the door; pieces "k", "l" and "m" in that order. Then the windows, "n" and "o".

* Press the seam allowances under on all sides for the windows before stitching them to the background fabric.

blindstitch

10. Using bias strip pattern piece "p" to make 0.6 cm [¼"] bias tape for the roof, position and pin in place; blindstitch (see step 13 on p. 54). This completes the block for House C.

Directions - House D

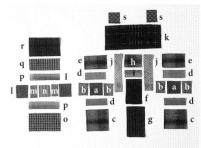

1. Do not add any seam allowance to pattern piece "f". Add a 0.3-0.5 cm [⅛"~¼"] seam allowance to pattern piece "s" and 0.7 cm [¼"] to all other pieces.

Segment A

0.3 [⅛"]

finished sewing line

2. Use the reverse appliqué technique by cutting away the design area from pattern piece "g" (leaving seam allowance as shown).

3. With right side out, center pattern piece "f" behind "g" and pin the fabrics together.

4. In each corner of the windows, clip the seam allowance to the corner at an angle, being careful not to cut through the finished sewing line.

5. Blindstitch the window openings to piece "f" by using the tip of the needle to turn the seam allowance under just to the finished sewing line as you sew.

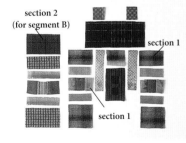

section 2 (for segment B)

section 1

section 1

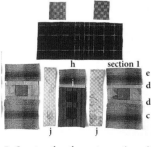

h section 1

e
d
d
c

j j

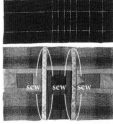

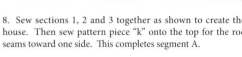

sew sew sew

sew

6. Sew the window pieces together in the following order: two sets of "b", "a" and "b"; 1 set of "l", "m", "n", "m" and "l". Sew section 2 together and both sections 1 together as shown above.

7. Sew together the center section with pieces "j", "h" and "i".

8. Sew sections 1, 2 and 3 together as shown to create the base of the house. Then sew pattern piece "k" onto the top for the roof. Press the seams toward one side. This completes segment A.

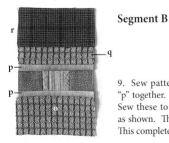

r

q

p

p

o

Segment B

9. Sew pattern pieces "o" and "p" and "q" and "p" together. Press the seams toward "o" and "p". Sew these to the section 2 piece made in step 6 as shown. Then, sew pattern piece "r" to the top. This completes segment B.

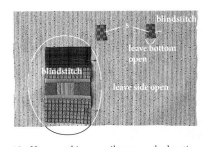

10. Use a marking pencil to trace the location of the appliqué onto the background fabric. Sew pieces "s" in place using a blindstitch. Turn under and press seam allowances for segment B on the edges that will not be overlapped by other pieces. Stitch onto the background.

11. Turn under and press seam allowances for segment A. Stitch in place as shown, overlapping segment B and the chimneys. Don't stitch the bottom edge.

Directions - House E

1. Cut patterns for piecing, "a", "g" and "k" with a 0.7 cm [¼"] seam allowance; the appliqué pieces and the 1.1 cm [⅜"] bias strip with a 0.3-0.5 cm [⅛"~¼"] seam allowance.

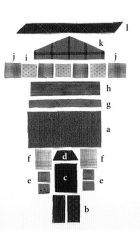

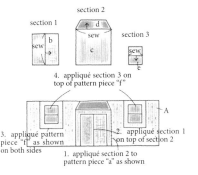

2. Refer to the diagram above and make the window and door sections. Appliqué them onto segment A as shown. For segments B and C, sew the specified pattern pieces together, pressing the seams to one side (refer to the arrows for pressing seam allowance directions).

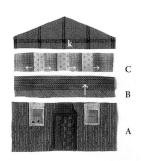

3. As shown above, sew segments A, B and C together, along with pattern piece "k" to complete the house block.

4. Turn under and press the seam allowance on the left and right sides; sew to the background fabric. Taking the prepared bias tape, piece "l", and stitch in place along the roofline (see p. 54). This completes the block for House E.

4. Finishing the quilt top.

1. Sew the five house blocks together as shown. Press the seams all in one direction.

2. Design and appliqué trees, fences or other elements onto the piece as you desire. (see p. 72 and 78 for detailed directions on appliquéing trees and fences).

3. To make the appliqué piece for the street, draw, freehand, a slightly curvy line toward the top of the 7 cm [2¾"] wide brown print fabric. Place it at the bottom of the pieced blocks and pin in place. Carefully, trim along the drawn line leaving a 0.3 cm [⅛"] seam allowance.

* When drawing the line for the street, think about the width of the street and the height of the houses. The finished height of the piece is 28 cm [11"], however, you can adjust this to whatever overall size is to your taste.

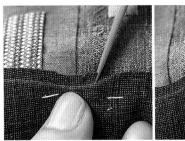

4. Clip the seam allowance at the inner curves. Use the tip of the needle to turn the seam allowance under as you blindstitch the street to the background.

5. Using embroidery thread and an outline stitch, stitch around the windows and doors to make them stand out. Make a French knot for the door knob. The quilt top is now complete and ready for quilting.

5. Basting and quilting.

1. Use a marking pencil to draw quilting lines on each of the houses and other elements. There is no need to mark the background as you will quilt this to look like wind currents flowing through the air (see the dimensional diagram on p. 51).

*   To draw quilting lines on the fabric, use either a regular soft-lead pencil for light fabrics or a chalk pencil for dark fabrics. Relax your hand and grip as you draw lightly on the fabric to get the look you desire.

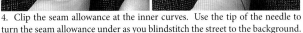
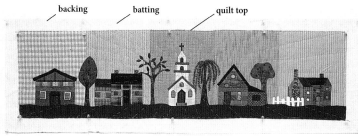

backing   batting   quilt top

2. Smooth out the backing fabric, right side down, on a flat surface and pin or tape to hold it taut. With the batting cut to the same size as the backing, lay it on top of the backing and re-pin or tape both layers to the flat surface. Center the quilt top on top of the layers and pin down. Baste.

* Basting Tips
Starting in the center of the quilt top with a length of knotted thread, baste to the left edge. Knot the thread at the edge and cut it, leaving a 2-3 cm [¾"~1¼"] tail. Start again in the center and baste out to the right edge. Starting in the center, next baste vertically out to the edges on the top and bottom borders; repeat at a diagonal to all four corners. Finally, baste completely around the edges.

For easier basting, use a spoon to help lift the needle from the surface of the quilt as you baste.

3. Place the inner ring of the quilting hoop on a flat surface; lay the area that you want to work on over it. Place the outer hoop over the inner hoop and firmly push down, so that the quilt sandwich is caught between the inner and outer hoop.

4. The quilt should be relaxed enough to be able to feel the table underneath when you press on the edge of the quilt inside the hoop. Tighten the screw.

5. See p. 76 for proper finger placement of the quilting notions. Rest the hoop in place between the edge of the table and your abdomen; begin to quilt. Move the hoop as needed to finish quilting. When complete, remove all basting thread except those around the edge.

Using thimbles

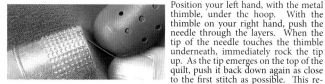

Position your left hand, with the metal thimble, under the hoop. With the thimble on your right hand, push the needle through the layers. When the tip of the needle touches the thimble underneath, immediately rock the tip up. As the tip emerges on the top of the quilt, push it back down again as close to the first stitch as possible. This repeated rocking motion is used for the most precise quilting stitches.

Quilting Step by Step

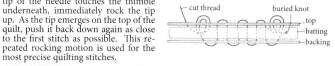

Beginning quilting stitches

1. Knot the end of the thread and insert the needle into the quilt top and batting about 2 cm [¾"] away from where you will begin the first stitch. Bring the tip of the needle up and exit at the exact spot for the first stitch without going through the backing.

2. Pull the thread through until the knot is lying on the surface of the quilt top. Gently tug the thread to pop the knot through the quilt top to bury it in the batting. Take another stitch at the exact place where you started.

3. Insert the needle again at the first stitch perpendicular to the top and pull through the back, coming up very close to the first stitch. Insert the needle down again until you feel the tip of the needle with your finger under the quilt and immediately come back up. Repeat this rocking motion until you have several stitches on your needle. Then use the thimble to push the needle through the quilt. Pull the thread to even the tension. Repeat until the end of your quilting line.

Ending quilting stitches

1. To finish off your quilting stitches, bring the needle up in the spot where you want the last stitch to be, leaving a space the width of two stitches between.

2. Backstitch into the preceding space that was left open, bringing the needle up to create a final stitch.

3. Insert the needle in the last stitch again and work the needle through the batting, bringing the tip of the needle out about 2 cm [¾"] away from the last stitch. Carefully cut the thread close to the quilt top.

Quilting Order

1) Quilt as desired inside of each house.
2) Quilt around each house and any other design element that has been added to outline them.
3) Quilt the background fabric in a pattern to look like wind currents.
4) Quilt the street, following the curves.

6. Binding the edges.

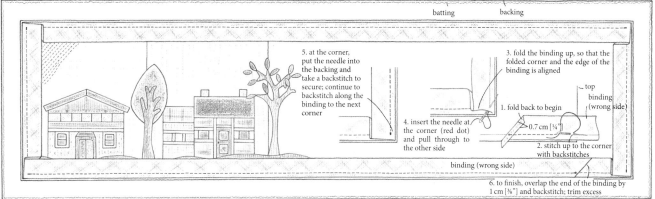

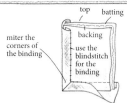

miter the corners of the binding
use the blindstitch for the binding

1. Make a 3.5 × 310 cm [1⅜" × 118"] bias binding (see p. 66).
2. Draw the finished sewing line all around the edge on the right side of the quilt top. Align the marked finished sewing line on the binding with the finished sewing line on the quilt top; pin in place. Refer to steps 1~6 in the diagram for binding directions.
3. Trim the excess seam allowance from the quilt top to match that of the binding (0.7 cm [¼"]). Bind the raw edges, and sew the binding down to the back of the quilt using the blindstitch.

Bag: **Stairs**

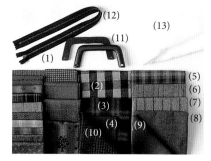

Shown on p. 7

- The full-size template/pattern can be found on Side A of the pattern sheet inserts.
- Finished measurement: 19.5 cm [7⅝"](w) × 30 cm [11¾"](h); 8 cm [3⅛"] gusset

Materials Needed

Homespuns
(1) Assorted fat quarters or scraps (piecing and appliqué)
(2) Large plaid - 10 × 42 cm [4" × 16½"] (zipper opening A)
(3) Plaid homespun - 15 × 20 cm [6" × 7⅞"] (gusset B)
(4) Brown print - 10 × 10 cm [4" × 4"] (tabs)
(5) Small check homespun - 110 × 30 cm [43¼" × 11¾"]
   (backing, gusset binding)
(6) Grey homespun - 25 × 70 cm [9⅞" × 27½"] (background A)
(7) Grey homespun - 15 × 70 cm [6" × 27½"] (background B)
(8) Grey homespun - 17 × 70 cm [6¾" × 27½"] (background C)

(9) Dk grey homepun - 15 × 15 cm [6" × 6"] (handle
   loops); 4 × 153 cm [1½" × 60¼"] (binding)
(10) Black homespun - 3.5 × 88 cm [1⅜" × 33⅞"] (zipper
   binding)
(11) Handles - 1 pair
(12) 1 Zipper - 39 cm [15⅜"]
(13) Batting - 110 × 30 cm [43¼" × 11¾"]
Other materials:
Fusible interfacing - 6 × 12 cm [2⅜" × 4¾"]

* Contrasting thread has been used in the
photos for instructional purposes.

Dimensional Diagram

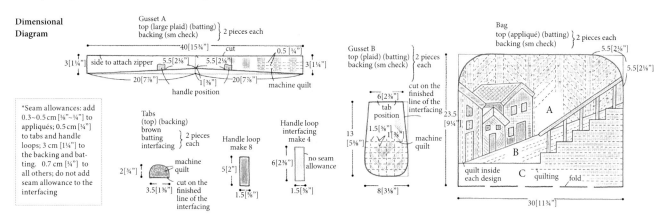

*Seam allowances: add 0.3~0.5 cm [⅛"~¼"] to appliqués; 0.5 cm [¼"] to tabs and handle loops; 3 cm [1¼"] to the backing and batting. 0.7 cm [¼"] to all others; do not add seam allowance to the interfacing

Gusset A
top (large plaid) (batting)
backing (sm check) } 2 pieces each
40[15¾"]   cut   0.5 [¼"]
3[1¼"] side to attach zipper 5.5[2⅛"] 5.5[2⅛"] 3[1¼"]
20[7⅞"]   1[⅜"] 20[7⅞"]
machine quilt
handle position

Tabs
(top) (backing)
brown
batting
interfacing } 2 pieces each
machine quilt
2[¾"]
cut on the finished line of the interfacing
3.5[1⅜"]

Handle loop
make 8
5[2"]
1.5[⅝"]

Handle loop
interfacing
make 4
no seam allowance
6[2⅜"]
1.5[⅝"]

Gusset B
top (plaid) (batting)
backing (sm check) } 2 pieces each
6[2⅜"]
tab position
cut on the finished line of the interfacing
1.5[⅝"] 1[⅜"]
machine quilt
13[5⅛"] 23.5[9¼"]
8[3⅛"]

Bag
top (appliqué) (batting)
backing (sm check) } 2 pieces each
5.5[2⅛"]
5.5[2⅛"]
A
B
quilt inside each design
C quilting
fold
30[11¾"]

1. Making the top.

* Mark the finished sewing line on the right side of the appliqué pieces and cut them with a 0.3~0.5 cm [⅛"~¼"] seam allowance. Add 0.7 cm [¼"] to piecing.

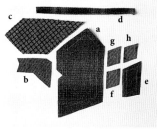

blindstitch

leave open

1. Create segment 1 by sewing pieces "a", "b" and "c" together. Blindstitch bias strip "d" in place on the roofline (step 13, p. 54). Prepare appliqué pieces "e" to "h" and blindstitch them in place on piece "a".

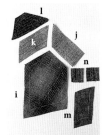

blindstitch

leave open

2. Create segment 2 by sewing pieces "j" and "k" together to make the roof. Next sew "i" and "l" to the roof section. Finally, appliqué the door and windows to the segment as shown.

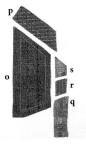

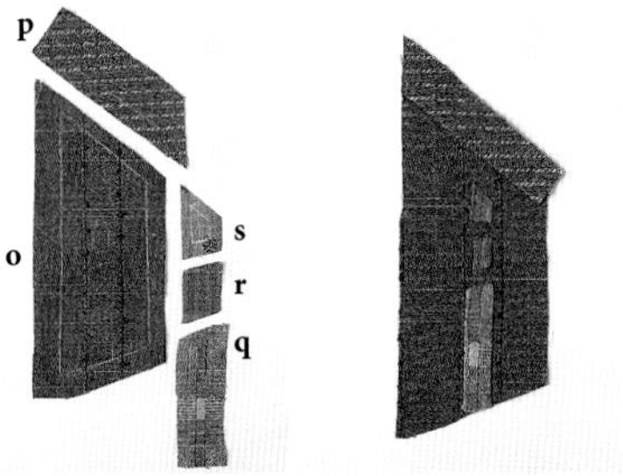

3. Create segment 3 by sewing pieces "o" and "p" together. Appliqué the windows and door to the segment.

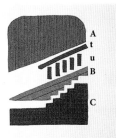

4. Cut background pieces A, B and C for the bag top. Then cut appliqué pattern pieces "t" and "u" for the stair railing.

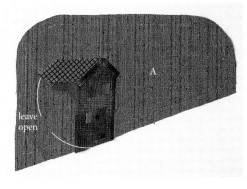

5. Draw the appliqué design onto background fabric A. Turn under and press the seam allowance of the roof and the right side of segment 1. Position in place and pin; blindstitch to the background. Leave the bottom and side open where other pieces will overlap.

6. Appliqué both segments 2 and 3, in turn, overlapping the segment before as shown.

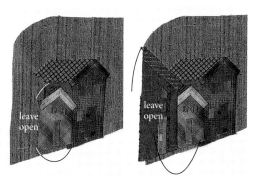

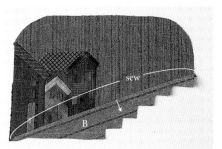

7. Sew background piece B to A from end to end. Press the seam allowance toward piece B.

8. Draw the appliqué design onto the background and appliqué pieces "u" (see steps 2~4, p. 55). Leave both the top and bottom of each rail open.

9. Next, appliqué the top of the railing, piece "t", in place, being sure to cover the tops of the rails.

2. Complete quilting and sew front/back together.

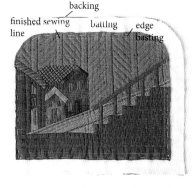

10. Appliqué background piece C to the piece finished in step 9. This completes one side of the bag. Repeat these steps to create the other side.

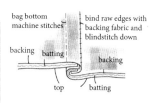

1. Using a marking pencil, draw quilting lines as shown (p. 60) or as desired. Layer quilt top and backing fabric with batting in between; baste. Use weights to hold down the quilt sandwich (see p. 68) and quilt inside the houses, around each design, and on the background. Remove all basting thread except for that around the edge. Make a template of the finished size of the bag and draw the finished sewing line around the edges on the right side.

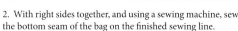

2. With right sides together, and using a sewing machine, sew the bottom seam of the bag on the finished sewing line.

3. Trim the top and batting down to 0.7 cm [¼"] seam allowance. Fold the backing and use to bind the raw edges; blindstitch down.

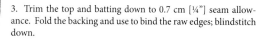

3. Making the zipper opening and gusset.

* If a 39 cm [15⅜"] zipper is not available, shorten a longer zipper to the desired length. See p. 65 on how to shorten a zipper.

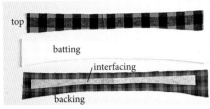

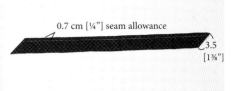

1. To create the zipper opening A, iron the fusible interfacing to the wrong side of the backing piece. Layer the batting and the top piece on top; baste. Machine quilt in 0.5 cm [¼"] intervals with thread that blends into the fabric.

2. Prepare two 3.5 × 44 cm [1⅜" × 17 ¼"] bias strips out of the small check fabric (5).

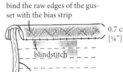

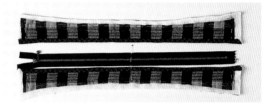

3. Use the bias strips from step 2 to bind the inside edges of the gusset as shown above (see p. 59).

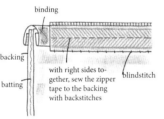

4. Use pins to mark the center point of the zipper.

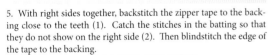

5. With right sides together, backstitch the zipper tape to the backing close to the teeth (1). Catch the stitches in the batting so that they do not show on the right side (2). Then blindstitch the edge of the tape to the backing.

6. Carefully unzip the zipper and using the same method, sew the other side of the zipper to the opening fabric A.

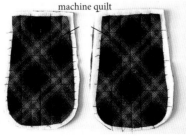

7. To create gusset B, iron the interfacing to the wrong side of the backing. Layer the batting and top; place on top of the backing; baste.

8. Machine quilt as shown or as desired with thread that blends into the fabric. Using the template, draw the finished sewing line on the backing.

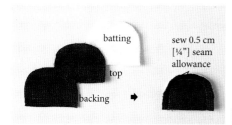

9. To create the tabs, place the top and backing with right sides together; lay on top of the backing; sew around the curves with a sewing machine.

10. Trim the batting close to the stitching. Find the template for the tab and cut it out of heavyweight paper or clear template plastic. Turn the tab over.

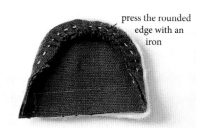

press the rounded edge with an iron

11. Sew a gathering stitch in the seam allowance and gather as shown; tie off. Place the template inside the rounded area and press the seam allowance well with an iron. Remove template.

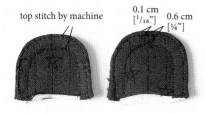

12. Turn the tabs right side out; top stitch as shown around curves. Make two tabs.

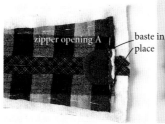

13. Center and position the tabs with raw edges even on either end of the zipper opening A. Baste them in place.

14. With right sides together and raw edges facing out, center both gusset B pieces on top of the zipper opening with basted tabs; pin. Machine stitch along the finished sewing lines.

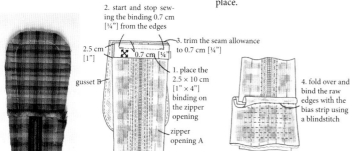

15. Trim the gusset seam allowance down to 0.7 cm [¼"]. Make bias strips with the backing fabric (5) and use it to bind the raw edges; blindstitch down.

This completes the gusset and zipper opening for the bag.

4. Making the handle loops.

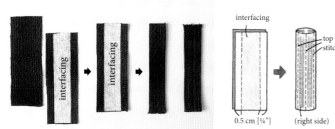

* When turning narrow tubes, using a tube turner makes it easier. See p. 66 for how to use a tube turner.

1. Cut out 8 handle loop pieces. Iron the interfacing to the center of the wrong side of four handle loop pieces. Take one piece with the interfacing and one piece without interfacing and with right sides together, sew along both edges with a sewing machine. Turn right side out and top stitch as shown in the illustration above. Make four handle loops.

2. Slip the loops through each of the four holes on the handles. Fold in half evenly and baste the ends together.

5. Finishing the bag.

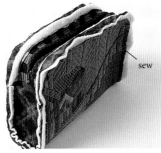

1. With wrong sides together and matching edges, align the center of the zipper opening with the center point on the bag top. Make sure the tabs are centered horizontally along both ends of the top of the bag. Pin in place all the way around on both sides, adjusting as necessary. Check for overall balance, with no tight or loose pinned areas. Sew on the marked finished sewing line with a sewing machine.

2. Baste the handle loops at the top of the zipper opening just outside the finished sewing line where specified (see dimensional diagram).

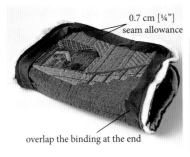

3. Make a 4×153 cm [1½" × 60¼"] bias binding. Draw a 0.7 cm [¼"] finished sewing line from the edge of the binding. Place it, with right sides together, against the bag. Pin, making sure that the finished sewing lines are aligned. Start and stop the binding, with overlap, at a point where it will be the least noticeable to the eye. Sew in place with a sewing machine.

4. Trim the excess seam allowance down to 0.7 cm [¼"] and align with the seam allowance of the binding.

5. Turn under 0.7 cm [¼"] on the raw edge of the binding and fold over the raw edge of the seam allowance. Pin it down in place against the gusset, easing around the curves.

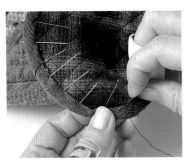

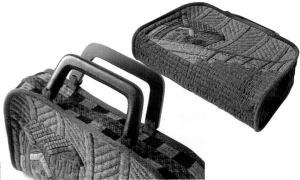

6. Using a blindstitch, sew the binding to the gusset fabric all the way around.

7. When you get to a handle loop, lift it up and stitch it together along with the binding so that the loop is attached to the binding and helps it to "stand up."

The completed bag.

How to shorten a zipper to the length you need.

- Use a zipper that is 1-1.5 cm [⅜"~⅝"] longer than the finished measurements.
- Tools needed: cutting nippers or pliers

1. Starting from the closed end, mark the zipper tape at the location of the desired length of the zipper.

2. Use the cutting nippers to remove about 2 cm [¾"] of teeth, starting at the marked location toward the top. Be sure not to remove the end teeth on both sides of the zipper tape at the top yet (see below).

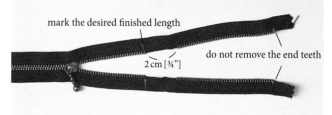

mark the desired finished length

do not remove the end teeth

2 cm [¾"]

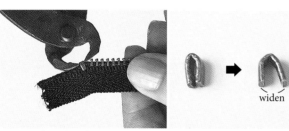

widen

3. Locate the end teeth at the top of the zipper. Use the cutting nippers to remove the end teeth on both sides and carefully open up the metal.

pinch end teeth to secure

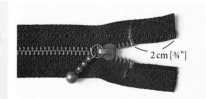

2 cm [¾"]

4. On each side, take the removed end teeth from step 3 and place them just next to the last tooth (at the area where you removed teeth). Use the pliers to pinch the end tooth tightly in place.

5. Cut the zipper tape, leaving 2 cm [¾"] from the end teeth.

Quilting terminology

Piecing - sewing fabric pieces (triangles, squares, etc.) together to create segments or blocks for a quilt top.
Blocks - units that are made up of piecing. Typically, a number of similar blocks sewn together create a quilt top.
Patterns - a design created by sewing fabric pieces or appliqués together.
Quilt top - the uppermost layer of fabric of a quilt, made up of pieces of different fabric that are sewn

together to create a pattern or picture.
Sashing - strips of fabric that are sewn between blocks.
Borders - strip(s) of fabric that frames the edge of the quilt.
Quilting lines - lines drawn on the fabric to assist in quilting patterns.
Quilt - a warm layer of batting enclosed between two layers of fabric and kept in place by lines of stitching.

Outline quilting - quilting right next to seam lines or appliqués to highlight the designs.
Pressing seams - in quilting, this refers to pressing the seam allowances to one side (usually toward the darker fabric). When pressing hand-pieced seams, leave 0.1 cm [¹/₁₆"] showing over the fold to hide the seam and press.
Binding - covering raw edges with a folded and stitched-down width of fabric on both the front and back. Most often made of bias fabric.

Using a tube turner to turn narrow fabric tubes right side out.

• This is a useful tool to turn narrow tubes used for handles or loops right side out. It can also be used with double layers when making fabric tubes with a facing inside.

1. Insert cylinder A through the fabric tube (wrong side out)

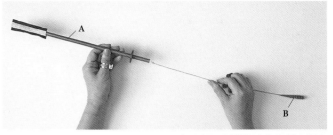

2. Slide the fabric tube down the cylinder until you have about 2 cm [¾"] to fold over. Insert wire B into cylinder A, as shown, and push the hook on the end of the wire through the folded fabric at the end. Twist it to get a good hold on the end of the fabric tube.

3. Carefully begin to pull the wire B back out of cylinder A, while sliding the fabric tube back along the cylinder. The fabric tube will be turning right side out inside the cylinder as it is being pulled through.

4. Once the entire fabric tube is through cylinder A, untwist the wire to release the hook from the end of the fabric tube.

Cutting and sewing bias fabric together

How to cut bias fabric

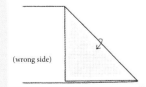

(wrong side)

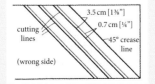

cutting lines

3.5 cm [1⅜"]
0.7 cm [¼"]
45° crease line

(wrong side)

1. Fold the fabric at a 45° angle and use your fingers to press the fold. Open the fabric back out.

2. Using your ruler and a marking pencil/chalk, draw a line along the crease. Using this as your reference line, continue to draw cutting lines in 3.5 cm [1⅜"] intervals. Then, with a different color, draw finished sewing lines 0.7 cm [¼"] inside the cutting lines. Cut apart.

How to sew bias fabric together

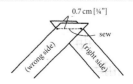

0.7 cm [¼"]
sew
(wrong side)
(right side)

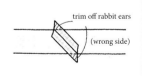

trim off rabbit ears
(wrong side)

1. With right sides together place two bias strips at an angle. Match the edges and pin; draw a line 0.7 cm [¼"] in from the edge. Sew the seam by machine, or if hand-sewing, use a backstitch for strength.

2. Open the seam (or to one side if hand-sewn) and press. Trim off the rabbit ears.

66

Handbag: A House Surrounded by Trees   Shown on p. 6

- The full-size template/pattern can be found on Side A of the pattern sheet inserts.
- Finished measurement: 23 cm [9"] (w) × 28 cm [11"] (h); 7 cm [2¾"] gusset

Materials Needed

Cottons

- Assorted fat quarters or scraps (piecing, appliqué)
- Homespun - 28 × 30 cm [11"×11¾"] (top - back)
- Plaid homespun - 35 × 80 cm [13¾"× 31½"]
  (backing, handle backing, bias to bind gusset)
- Homespun - 3.5 ×60 cm [1⅜"×23⅝"] (binding)
- Homespun - 24 × 20 cm [9½"×7⅞"] (handle top, piecing)
- Batting - 35 ×80 cm [13¾"×31½"]
- Flannel - 24 ×10 cm [9½"×4"]

Seam allowances: add 0.3-0.5 cm [⅛"~¼"] to appliqué; 0.7 cm [¼"] to piecing; 3 cm [1¼"] to the backing and batting. Cut the handle fabric without any seam allowance.

Dimensional Diagram

Bag front - 1 piece each
top fabric (pieced top) (batting)
backing (plaid homespun)

binding   10 [1½"]   attach handles

0.7 [¼"]   binding

m

a *b c* *a*
d

e *f* *g*   *s*

l   *l*   26 [10¼"]

h
i *j* *k*
r   *q*

n   *p*   *o*

28 [11"]

Bag back - 1 piece each
top fabric (homespun) (batting)
backing (plaid homespun)

crosshatch quilt the background - 1.5 cm [⅝"]

28 [11"]

Handles - 2 pieces each
top fabric (homespun)
backing (plaid homespun)
(batting) (flannel)

24 [9⅜"]

5 [2"]

1. Cutting out individual pieces.

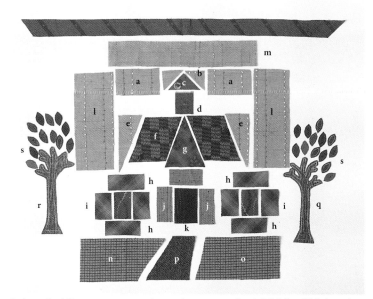

Refer to the full-size patterns to make templates. For appliqués "q", "r" and "s", draw their finished sewing lines on the right side and cut them with a 0.3-0.5 cm [⅛"~¼"] seam allowance. Cut the other pattern pieces with a 0.7 cm [¼"] seam allowance. Make a 3.5 × 60 cm [1⅜"× 23⅝"] binding.

2. Making the top

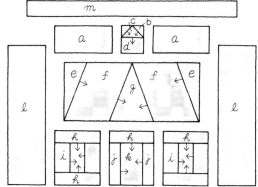

1. Sew all of the pattern pieces of the house together to make the units as shown in the diagram above. Press the seam allowances in the direction indicated by the arrows in the diagram.

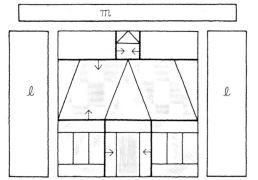

2. Sew the units together for the block that makes up the bag front.

67

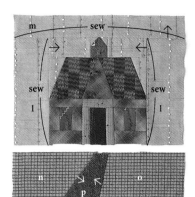

3. Sew pattern pieces "l" to the right and left sides of the center house block, and pattern piece "m" to the top. Press the seam allowances in the direction indicated by the arrows in the diagram. Sew the path pattern pieces, "n", "p" and "o", together as shown. Press the seam allowance toward pattern piece "p".

4. Appliqué trees onto the completed house block. Then sew the path to the bottom of the house. Press the seam allowance toward the path. This completes the top for the front of the bag.

3. Quilting

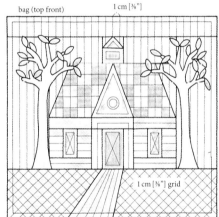

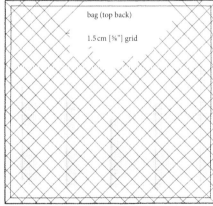

1. Use a marking pencil to draw quilting lines on both the top front and top back of the bag.

2. Layer the backing and top front with batting in between; baste (see p. 58).

3. Place the thimbles and quilting tools on both hands (see p. 76). Place the quilt top on the edge of a table and hold it in place using a weight. Start quilting from the center of the piece toward the outer edges (see p. 59). Then layer and baste the bag top back. Quilt an overall pattern as shown above, or as desired. Remove all the basting thread except for those around the very edges.

Tip: If the quilt sandwich is too small to easily hoop, use a weight to hold it in place.

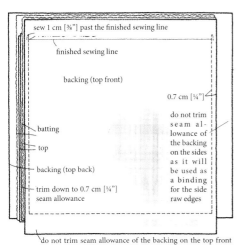

sew 1 cm [⅜"] past the finished sewing line

finished sewing line

backing (top front)

0.7 cm [¼"]

do not trim seam allowance of the backing on the sides as it will be used as a binding for the side raw edges

batting

top

backing (top back)

trim down to 0.7 cm [¼"] seam allowance

do not trim seam allowance of the backing on the top front bottom as it will be used as a binding for the raw edges

1. With right sides together and using a sewing machine, sew the top front and top back together along the sides and the bottom. Trim the seam allowance down to 0.7 cm [¼"], leaving the backing for the top back on the sides and the backing for the top front on the bottom.

2. Do not bind 3.5 cm [1⅜"] on the corners where you will make the gusset.

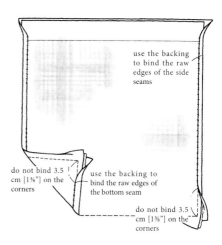

use the backing to bind the raw edges of the side seams

do not bind 3.5 cm [1⅜"] on the corners

use the backing to bind the raw edges of the bottom seam

do not bind 3.5 cm [1⅜"] on the corners

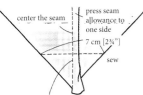

center the seam

press seam allowance to one side

7 cm [2¾"]

sew

1. Center the seam on the side of the bag and fold the corner tip into a triangle. With the triangle flattened down, use a marking pencil to draw a line 7 cm [2¾"] across. Sew across the line to create a gusset.

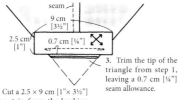

seam

9 cm [3½"]

2.5 cm [1"]   0.7 cm [¼"]

3. Trim the tip of the triangle from step 1, leaving a 0.7 cm [¼"] seam allowance.

2. Cut a 2.5 × 9 cm [1"× 3½"] bias strip from the backing fabric to make the binding. With right sides together, sew the gusset and bias together along the finished sewing line.

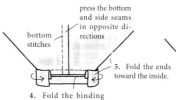

press the bottom and side seams in opposite directions

bottom stitches

5. Fold the ends toward the inside.

4. Fold the binding over the raw edge.

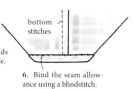

bottom stitches

6. Bind the seam allowance using a blindstitch.

bind side seams

bottom seam

3. Refer to the diagrams above to make the gussets.

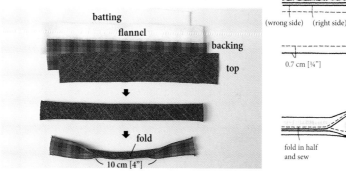

batting

flannel

backing

top

fold

10 cm [4"]

batting   flannel

(wrong side)   (right side)

0.7 cm [¼"]

top stitch   0.6 cm [¼"]

3.5 cm [1⅜"]

fold in half and sew

4. To make the handles, with right sides together, layer the backing and top fabric. Layer the flannel and the batting against the wrong side of the backing and sew along edges lengthwise. Trim the batting and flannel and turn right side out. Press and top stitch double lines on each edge. Fold the center 10 cm [4"] and top stitch the edge. Make 2.

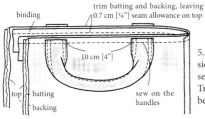

binding

trim batting and backing, leaving 0.7 cm [¼"] seam allowance on top

10 cm [4"]

top   batting

backing

sew on the handles

5. Baste the handles to the inside. With right sides together, sew the binding to the opening. Trim the batting and flannel to be even with the binding.

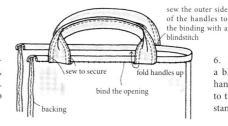

sew the outer side of the handles to the binding with a blindstitch

sew to secure   fold handles up

bind the opening

backing

6. Bind the opening using a blindstitch. Lift up the handles and sew the handles to the binding to secure in a standing position.

Quilt: **Block of the Month I** Shown on p. 42

- The house and fence patterns can be found on Side D of the pattern sheet inserts.
- Finished measurement: 183.4 cm [72¼"] (w) × 180.4 cm [71"] (h)

Materials Needed

Cottons
- 24 assorted fat quarters or scraps (background, piecing, appliqué for house blocks)
- Assorted fat quarters or scraps (fence appliqué on border)
- Beige homespun - 11 × 140 cm [4⅜" × 55⅛"] (sashing A - sky)
- Brown homespun - 11 × 140 cm [4⅜" × 55⅛"] (sashing B - ground)
- Medium brown homespun - 18 × 145 cm [7" × 57⅛"] (inner border C and D)
- Taupe print - 80 × 181 cm [31½" × 71¼"] (outer border A and B)
- Neutral print - 110 × 390 cm [43¼" × 4⅓ yds] (backing)
- Check print - 3.5 × 730 cm [1⅜" × 8 yds.] (binding)
- Batting - 195 × 190 cm [77" × 75"]

Tips for putting the 24 blocks together:

1. After all the blocks are completed, lay them out in 5 rows (see dimensional diagram). Try not to have similar house shapes next to each other.

2. If you need to add fabric in between the blocks so that each of the 5 rows is of an equal length, use the same background fabric as one of the blocks on either side. Sew that strip to the side of the house block (as shown below).

3. Before sewing the rows together, use a design wall to make sure you are happy with the overall balance. Then sew the sashing strips to the top (sashing A - sky) and bottom (sashing B - ground) of each row before sewing the rows together.

Dimensional Diagram

A= pattern   B = pattern variation

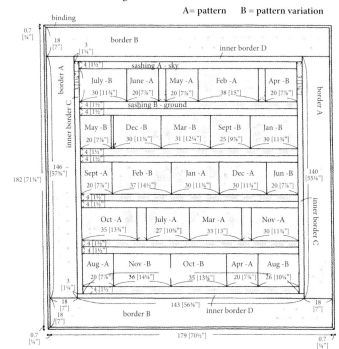

Seam allowances: add 0.3-0.5 cm [⅛"~¼"] to appliqué; 0.7 cm [¼"] to piecing; 3 cm [1¼"] to the backing and batting.

1. Cutting out individual pieces.

July -B   June - A   May - A   Feb - A   Apr -B

1. Using the dimensional diagram as a guide, lay the 24 houses out, creating each of the 5 rows. Add fabric strips in between the blocks, if needed, so that all 5 rows are the same length.

2. Sew the blocks together. If sewing by hand, use a backstitch at the beginning and end to secure. Press the seam allowances to one side.

3. Decide what other design elements you want to add to each row. Cut out the tree or other pattern pieces and appliqué them to the background. Add any embroidery desired to enhance the quilt.

70

Second Row

Third Row

Fourth Row

Fifth Row

4. Put rows 2-5 together using the same process as described in steps 1-3. Add appliqué and embroidery as desired.

Tip: Feel free to create your own variations for the buildings. For example, the house 4th from the left on the 3rd row is a combination of the September house, replacing the middle section of the February house.

3. Lay the single sashing strips "A" and "B" and the sashing "A•B" sets between each of the 5 rows. Make sure they are all of equal length.

2. Sewing the center of the quilt.

1. Cut the sashing strips that go between each of the 5 rows. Use the beige (sashing A) to create the sky at the top of each of the 5 rows. Use the brown (sashing B) to create the ground on the bottom of each of the 5 rows.

2. Sew 4 sets of sashing "A" and "B" together, as shown above. You will have one sashing "A" and one sashing "B" left over.

4. Sew the single sashing A strip to the top of row 1 and the remaining single sashing B to the bottom of row 5. Then sew the sashing sets to the house block rows, being sure that the "ground" is under the houses and the "sky" is above the houses. Press the seam allowances toward the sashing.

inner border D

inner border C

5. Refer to the dimensional diagram to cut the inner border strips "C" and "D".

6. Sew the inner border "C" to each side, followed by the inner border "D" to the top and bottom. Press the seam allowances toward the borders.

3. Appliquéing the fence to the border.

• The fences are created free form. Design the width, height and spacing as you desire.

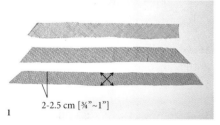

2-2.5 cm [¾"~1"]

1

2

1. Refer to the dimensional diagram to cut the borders "A" and "B". Decide on the size and design of the fencing. Cut out the strips for the fence (using 2-2.5 cm [¾"~1"]. Bias strips will be easier to work with when appliquéing).

2. Use a marking pencil to draw rough locations for the 2 horizontal fencing pieces between each post on each border. Each should be approximately 5-6 cm [2"~2⅜"] above the other.

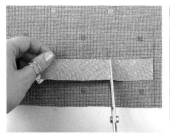

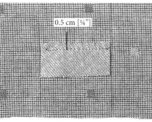

0.5 cm [¼"]

3. Cut the bias strip to equal the length of the horizontal fencing. Lay it with right sides together to the border fabric.

4. Align the finished sewing line to the marking pencil line on the border fabric. Backstitch along the finished sewing line.

5. Flip the fence piece up, and using the tip of your needle, turn the seam allowance under; finger press. Pin in place and blindstitch to the background.

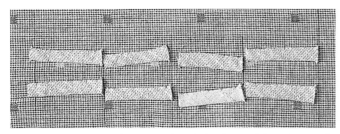

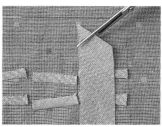

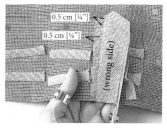

6. Appliqué the remaining fence pieces along the borders on all four sides. It will appear more rustic if you appliqué these free form in slightly different angles and widths.

7. Cut 2.5-3.5 cm [1"~1⅜"] bias strips for the fence posts. Place them vertically to cover the raw edges of the horizontal fence pieces and align to the bottom of the border. Cut the tip as shown above.

8. As you did for the fence pieces, sew along the finished sewing line on one side. Trim the opposite side to create uneven posts.

leave open

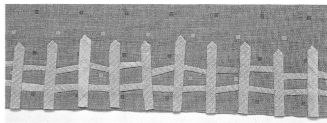

9. Flip the fence post piece over and using the tip of your needle, turn the seam allowance under; finger press and pin in place. Blindstitch up to the tip of the post, take a backstitch to secure at the tip and then stitch back down to form the triangle at the top of the fence post. Blindstitch the rest of the post to the bottom.

10. Do not appliqué all the way to the end of the border fabrics or the corner areas (see photo below). These will be completed after the borders are sewn onto the center section of the quilt top.

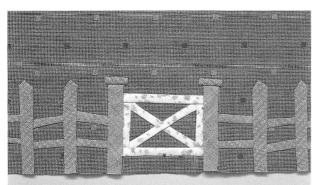

11. Appliqué gate posts and gates as shown, or where desired. To make the fencing continuous around the corners, angle the fence pieces and posts at both ends of border B (top and bottom).

4. Sewing on the borders and finishing the top.

1. Sew borders "A" to the right and left sides of the center pieced top (1), making sure the fencing is facing the correct way. Then sew borders "B" (2) to the top and bottom. Press the seam allowances toward the sashing strips.

2. Appliqué the remaining fencing pieces on the corners to connect the fencing all the way around. This completes the quilt top.

3. Appliquéing the fence to the border.

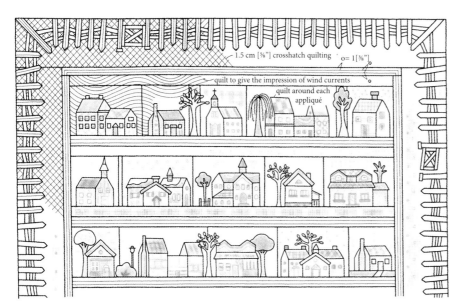

1.5 cm [⅝"] crosshatch quilting   o= 1[⅜"]

quilt to give the impression of wind currents

quilt around each appliqué

1. With a marking pencil and ruler, draw a crosshatch pattern on the border background and straight lines on the sashing strips.

2. Smooth out the backing fabric (wrong side up) on a flat surface and pin or tape to hold it taut. With the batting cut to the same size as the backing, lay it on top of the backing and re-pin or tape both layers to the flat surface. Center the quilt top on top of the layers and pin down.

4. With a relaxed hand, free form draw wind currents in each house block background. Use chalk for dark backgrounds and a soft lead pencil for lighter background fabrics.

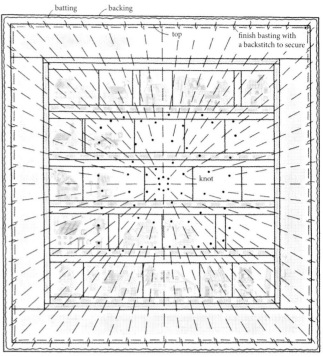

3. Starting in the center of the quilt top with a length of knotted thread, baste to the left edge. Backstitch at the end and knot the thread; cut it leaving a 2-3 cm [¾~1½"] tail. Start again at the center and baste out to the right edge. Then baste vertically to the top and to the bottom. Repeat this diagonally as shown above. No wide spaces should be left unbasted so that the layers do not shift during quilting.

Basting Order

Be sure to always baste from the center outwards to keep the layers smooth.
The general rule is that all basting lines should be no more than about a (hand) palm apart.

1. Center horizontal and vertical lines.
2. Diagonal lines all fanning out from the center.
3. Between the already-basted diagonal lines closer to the outer edge.
4. Around the entire edge of the quilt.

How to make a large backing

To make a backing that is larger than the width of the fabric, sew two pieces together along the selvage sides (after trimming it) to get the required width. If machine sewn, press the seam open. If sewn by hand, use a running stitch and press the seam to one side.

Basic Hand Sewing Stitches

Running Stitch

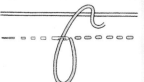

Backstitch (single)

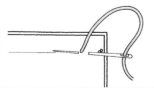

Backstitch (continuous)

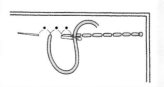

Blindstitch

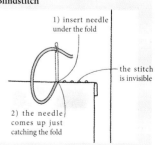

1) insert needle under the fold

2) the needle comes up just catching the fold

the stitch is invisible

6. Using a quilting frame.

I always use a quilting frame if I am quilting a large quilt as it is easier to work with the quilt sandwich. However, if you do not have a frame, a large quilting hoop will work just fine.

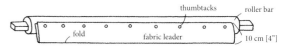

1. Attach a very strong fabric (such as canvas) to the frame, using thumbtacks to secure it to the roller bar. Repeat for the other roller bar. These become the leaders of the frame, to which you attach your quilt sandwich.

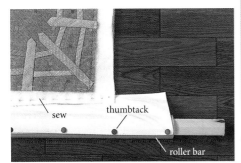

2. Align and center the edge of the quilt sandwich on the fabric leader; baste to the leader. Making sure that the quilt is laying straight, repeat this by attaching the opposite end of the quilt to the other leader.

3. Having someone help you, roll the quilt over the roller bars evenly from both sides so that the very center of the quilt is showing between the bars.

4. Insert the roller bars into the grooves on the quilting frame. Make eight smaller fabric leaders, 5 × 20 cm [2" × 7⅞"] for the sides. Secure the ends to the wood of the quilt frame with thumbtacks at equal intervals (four leaders on each side). Pin the side edges of the quilt sandwich to these side leaders so that the quilt stays taut in the frame.

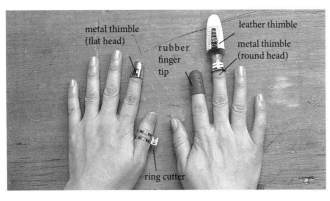

5. As shown in the photograph to the left, use these tools to protect your fingers while quilting.

6. Find a chair or stool that will position you at a comfortable height as you lean over the quilting frame. Thread a quilting between needle with the color that you desire. I usually pick a color that will blend in well with the color of fabric I am working on. Begin to quilt from the center and work your way out. You should try to take approximately 3 stitches in 1 cm [⅜"]. It is ideal to have the same size stitches showing on both the front and back of your work. Once you have completed quilting the center section, remove the side leader pins and roll the quilt to move on to the next section to quilt. Put it back in the quilting frame, re-pin and continue to quilt.

Quilting Order
1. Quilt as desired inside of each house.
2. Quilt around each house and any other design element that has been added.
3. Quilt the background fabric and sashing A in a pattern to imitate wind currents.
4. Quilt the surrounding sashing B.
5. Quilt inside and around the fencing.
6. Quilt the borders.

7. Binding your quilt.

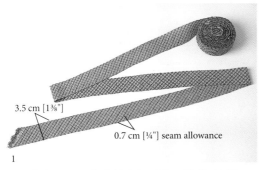

3.5 cm [1⅜"]

0.7 cm [¼"] seam allowance

1

2

1. Cut the homespun check fabric into 3.5 cm [1⅜"] wide bias strips. Sew the strips together to equal approximately 730 cm [8 yds]. Draw a 0.7 cm [¼"] seam allowance line on the wrong side.

2. Remove all the basting stitches, except for those around the edge. Draw the finished sewing line on the right side of the quilt top.

3

backstitch fold back 0.7 cm [¼"]

4

3. Begin binding the quilt near the corner of one side where it will be least noticeable to the eye. With right sides together, align the finished sewing line of the quilt top and the marked seam allowance line of the binding. Folding the end of the binding back 0.7 cm [¼"] at the beginning, pin all the way to the first corner.

4. Backstitch along the sewing line and stop 0.7 cm [¼"] in from the end, pushing the needle through to the backing.

5

6

5. Fold the binding up at a 45° angle and pin in place to hold. Then pin the binding along the side up to the next corner.

6. Taking the threaded needle, insert it into the corner of the binding coming out to the other side.

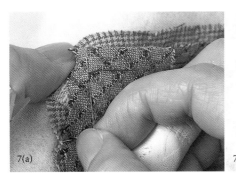

7(a)

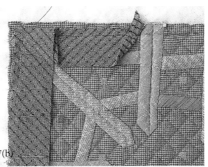

7(b)

7. Backstitch right at the point where you just brought the needle through to secure (a). Then, using a backstitch, continue to sew along the side to the next corner (b). Repeat steps 3~7 above until you reach the starting point.

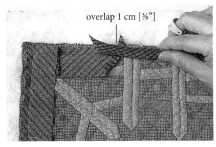

overlap 1 cm [⅜"]

8. To finish the binding, overlap the binding over the folded starting point; trim, so that the overlapping binding is 1 cm [⅜"]. Stitch it down to the end.

9. Trim the excess seam allowance from the edge of the quilt, so that the backing and batting are even with the edges of top and binding.

10. Turn the quilt over and fold the binding from the front to the back. Fold the seam allowance under and cover the raw edges; pin the binding in place around the entire quilt. Blindstitch the binding to the backing, starting where the binding overlapped in step 8.

How to appliqué trees.

A - appliquéd leaves

For detailed instructions on appliquéing around the curves of the trunk and leaves, refer to p. 53. Trace and cut out the appliqué patterns and pieces. Using a blindstitch, appliqué the trunk to the background fabric, followed by the leaves.

B - embroidered leaves

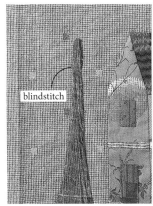

blindstitch

outline stitch

lazy daisy stitch

1. Position and pin the trunk in place. Using a blindstitch, sew it to the background fabric, turning the seam allowance under with the tip of the needle as you work.

2. Use a marking pencil to draw the branches. Embroider the base of the branches with an outline stitch, using two strands of embroidery thread.

3. Embroider leaves evenly along the base of the branches, using a lazy daisy stitch (two strands).

Wall Quilt: **On a Street Corner** Shown on p. 44

• This is a variation of the Monthly Quilt shown on p. 42. Refer to that project for overall directions.
- Finished measurement: 194.4 × 164.4 cm [76⅜" × 64¾"]

Materials Needed
Cottons
- Assorted fat quarters or scraps (piecing, appliqué, background, and streets)
- Dk tan print - 12 × 165 cm [4¾" × 65"] (border D)
- Tan print - 90 × 165 cm [35⅜" × 65"] (border A, B, C)
- Plaid homespun - 3.5 × 725 cm [1⅜" × 8 yds] (bias binding)
- homespun - 110 × 350 cm [43¼" × 4 yd.] (backing)
- Batting - 250 × 175 cm [1¾ yd × 68⅞"]

Instructions

1. Trace and cut out all of the pieces for the various houses you desire from pattern sheet D. Piece them together.
2. Prepare the five center background sections, 33 × 109 cm [13" × 43"] by sewing assorted beige fabric pieces together.
3. Appliqué all of the houses onto the background sections from step 2, using a blindstitch (the trees and other elements will be added on later).
4. Cut the 5 sashing pieces for the streets (see p. 57) and appliqué them below each of the five house sections.
5. Sew the five house sections together in the order planned to create the large center of the quilt.
6. Trace and cut out all of the pieces for various houses and trees you desire to put around the border (A, B and C) from pattern sheet D. Piece them together and appliqué them to the three borders. Measure and cut out three inner border strips for the street to go along the three sides as well; appliqué them to the bottom of the three outer borders.
7. Sew the borders A and B to the sides of the center piece. Then sew border C to the top. Sew border D to the bottom. The quilt top is complete.
8. Using a marking pencil, draw quilting lines on the top. Layer the backing and quilt top with batting in between; baste. Quilt as desired.
9. Cut the plaid homespun into 3.5 cm [1⅜"] wide binding and bind the quilt (p. 59).

Dimensional Diagram

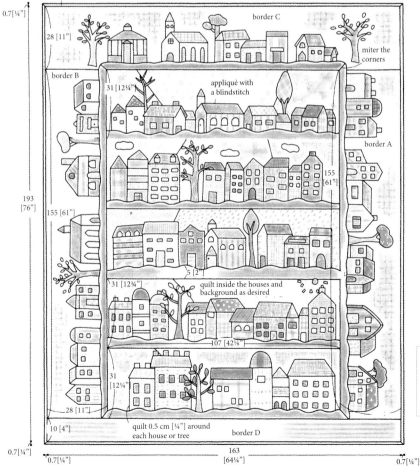

binding

top (appliqué) (batting)
backing (homespun)   } 1 piece each
binding (plaid)

0.7 [¼"]

28 [11"]

border C

border B

31 [12¼"]

appliqué with a blindstitch

miter the corners

border A

193 [76"]

155 [61"]

155 [61"]

quilt inside the houses and background as desired

5 [2"]

31 [12¼"]

107 [42⅛"]

31 [12¼"]

28 [11"]

10 [4"]

quilt 0.5 cm [¼"] around each house or tree

border D

0.7 [¼"]

0.7 [¼"]

163 [64¼"]

0.7 [¼"]

Seam allowances: add 0.3-0.5 cm [⅛"~¼"] to appliqué and piecing; 0.7 cm [¼"] to all other fabrics; prepare the backing and batting to be 205 × 175 cm [80¾" × 68⅞"].

Quilt: **The Chatter of Houses** Shown on p. 45

• This quilt is primarily free form and can be fun for a beginner.
• Finished measurement: 184.4 × 170.4 cm [72½" × 67"]

Materials Needed
Cottons
• Assorted fat quarters or scraps (piecing, appliqué, background, and streets)
• Charcoal grey print - 110 × 175 cm [43¼" × 69"] (border A)
• Dk grey print - 68 × 120 cm [26¾" × 47¼"] (border B)
• Tan homespun - 110 × 60 cm [43¼" × 23⅝"] (sashing)
• Beige print - 110 × 24 cm [43¼" × 9⅜"] (outer scallop border)
• Homespun - 3.5 × 710 cm [1⅜" × 8 yds] (bias binding)
• Homespun - 110 × 360 cm [43¼" × 4 yd.] (backing)
• Batting - 250 × 190 cm [1¾ yd × 74¾"]
• Embroidery thread - lt beige, other colors that you would like to use.

Instructions
1. All of the houses for this quilt are free form and as such, there are no patterns for them. Refer to p. 81 for directions on how to make your own houses.
2. Once all of your 49 house blocks for the center of the quilt are completed, measure (adding seam allowance) and cut sashing strips and sew them between the house blocks. Then cut 6 horizontal sashing strips and sew the strips together to create the center. Use the same fabric to make an inner border (see dimensional diagram below for exact measurements for each).
3. Measure and cut borders A and B; create free form houses and appliqué to the borders (see photo for spacing of houses). Appliqué the streets to the bottom of the borders (see p. 57). Design and appliqué trees, fences, and any other design elements

to the borders; embroider if desired.
4. Sew border B to the center block, starting with the sides, then the top and bottom. Sew border A to border B using the same process.
5. Cut the outer border into a free form scallop pattern and pin to the edge of border A. Turning the seam allowance under with the tip of your needle, appliqué it around the entire quilt using a blindstitch.
6. Using a colonial knot stitch (lt beige, 6 strands), embroider along the scalloped edge as shown (in photo). Continue to embroider over the entire quilt as desired, using colors and stitches that you prefer.
7. Layer the backing and quilt top with batting in between; baste. Quilt as desired.
8. Bind the quilt with a 3.5 cm [1⅜"] bias binding.

Dimensional Diagram

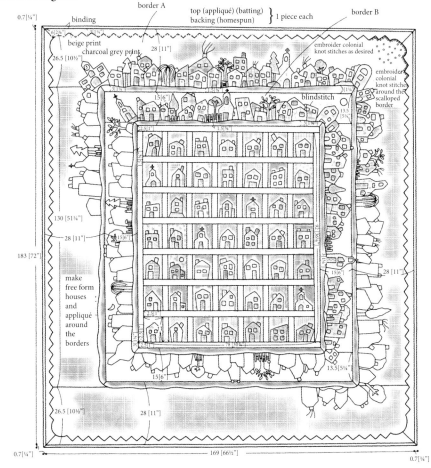

Colonial Knot Stitch

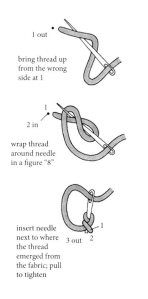

1 out
bring thread up from the wrong side at 1

2 in
wrap thread around needle in a figure "8"

insert needle next to where the thread emerged from the fabric; pull to tighten
3 out

Seam allowances: add 0.3-0.5 cm [⅛"~¼"] to appliqué and piecing; 0.7 cm [¼"] to all other fabrics; prepare the backing and batting to be 192 × 178 cm [75½" × 70⅛"].

How to make free form house blocks.

1. Cut a free form house shape out of fabric, including seam allowances. This is a scrappy quilt, so use any scrap or fabric that appeals to you.

2. Use a seam pressing tool to mark the seam allowances 0.3-0.5 cm [⅛"~¼"] for the appliqué pieces' finished shape. Do not turn under the bottom of the house as it will be sewn to the sashing.

3. Cut out the 10 × 12 cm [4" × 4¾"] background block. Mark the 0.5 cm [¼"] seam allowances around the edges. Position the house as desired and pin in place.

4. Cut out a chimney; turn the seam allowance under on all sides except the bottom. Using a marking pencil, draw the location of the chimney on the background fabric.

5. Removing house, blindstitch the three sides of the chimney in place.

6. Reposition the house, overlapping the bottom of the chimney. Appliqué the house to the background using the blindstitch.

7. Choose fabrics for the windows and door. Cut out size and shape that you desire.

8. Appliqué the windows and the door to the house using the blindstitch. Create each house for all 49 center blocks using this technique.

How to make bias binding.

* There are various sizes of bias tape makers. Buy the one that will equal the final bias tape or binding width that you need for your project.

1. Feed the bias strip into the bias tape maker right side up. Guide it along with a needle until it emerges from the other end.

2. Flip the bias tape maker upside down. Press the folded bias strip with the tip of the iron and gently pull the bias tape maker away from the iron. As you pull away, iron the folded bias strip that appears. Continue this along the entire length.

How to appliqué free form houses on the borders

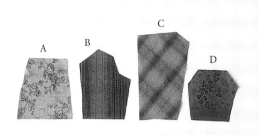

1. Cut a free form house shape out of fabric, including seam allowances.

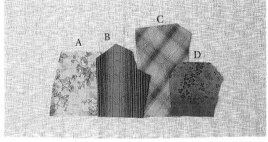

2. Position the houses on the border fabric, layering and overlapping them in the order you want .

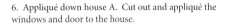

3. Cut out a chimney for house C; position in place on the background fabric. Leaving the bottom open, stitch the other three sides using a blindstitch.

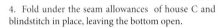

4. Fold under the seam allowances of house C and blindstitch in place, leaving the bottom open.

5. Cut out and appliqué windows to house C; cut out and appliqué a chimney for house A.

6. Appliqué down house A. Cut out and appliqué the windows and door to the house.

7. Cut out a chimney for house B and appliqué it in place. Then, appliqué the house, windows and door.

8. Appliqué house D last.

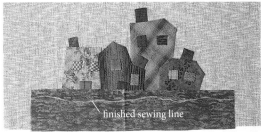

9

10

9. Cut the fabric for the street (p. 57) and position it in place under the houses. Use a marking pencil to draw, free-hand, a slightly curvy line.

10. Cut the fabric along the marked line, adding a 0.5 cm [¼"] seam allowance at the top. Blindstitch down. Make all the border houses in the same way.

Bag: **Storehouses in the Dark** Shown on p. 8

• The full-size template/pattern can be found on Side C of the pattern sheet inserts.
• Finished measurement: 36 cm [14⅛"] (w) × 29 cm [11⅜"] (h); 8 cm [3⅛"] gusset

Materials Needed

Cottons
- Two homespuns - 45×30 cm [17¾"×11¾"] (appliqué)
- Black homespun - 80 ×45 cm [31½"×17¾"] (top, lining for opening, handles)
- Dk homespun - 80×10 cm [31½"×4"] (gusset top)
- Plaid homespun - 45×110 cm [17¾"×43¼"] (backing, bias fabric for inside)
- Plaid homespun - 3.5×15 cm [1⅜"×6"] (bias binding)
- Batting - 85×45 cm [33½" ×17¾"]
- Fusible interfacing - 80×20 cm [31½" ×7⅞"]
- Handles - 1 pair
- Embroidery thread - dk beige, grey

Instructions

1. Referring to the full-size patterns and the dimensional diagram, cut out all of the pieces of fabric, batting and fusible interfacing for the bag, as well as the appliqué pieces for the design, adding specified seam allowances.
2. Appliqué and embroider the top according to the design. Layer the backing and top with the batting in between; baste. Quilt as shown or as desired.
3. Make the gusset by ironing the fusible interfacing to the backing fabric. Then, with wrong sides together, layer the top and backing with the batting in between; baste. Machine quilt as desired. Use the plaid homespun binding to bind the raw seams at the top section of each gusset.
4. With right sides together and matching center points and marks, pin the front and back of the bag and the gusset together. Machine sew the seams.
5. Iron the fusible interfacing to the wrong side of the lining pieces. With right sides together, sew them, matching marks, to the outside opening of each side of the bag. Clip the seam allowance around the curves and turn the lining to the inside of the bag against the backing. Turn under the seam allowance on the raw edge; blindstitch to the backing.
6. Following directions below, sew the handle lining and inside bias binding to the bag; attach handles and finish the bag.

Diagram 1 - How to attach the handles

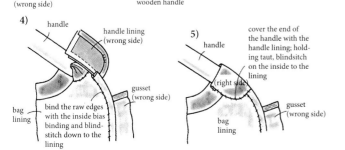

Dimensional Diagram

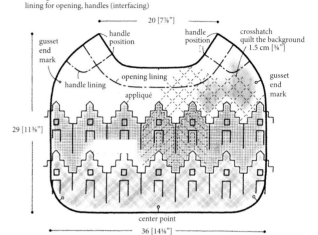

Bag - 2 pieces each
top fabric (appliquéd piece) (batting)
backing
lining for opening, handles (interfacing)

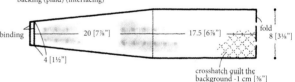

Gusset- 1 piece each
top fabric (black homespun) (batting)
backing (plaid) (interfacing)

Seam allowances: add 0.3-0.5 cm [⅛"~¼"] to appliqué; 0.7 cm [¼"] to top fabric; 3 cm [1¼"] to the backing and batting. Cut the interfacing without any seam allowance.

Finished Diagram

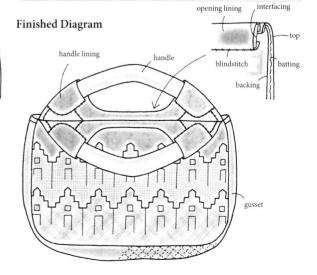

Bag: A General Store Shown on p. 10

- The full-size template/pattern can be found on Side A of the pattern sheet inserts.
- Finished measurement: 22.5 cm [8⅞"] (w) × 26 cm [10¼"] (h); 8 cm [3⅛"] gusset

Materials Needed

Cottons
- Assorted fat quarters or scraps (piecing, appliqué)
- Beige homespun - 30 × 50 cm [11¾" × 19¾"] (top, gusset B)
- Dk brown homespun - 12 × 40 cm [4¾" × 15¾"] (gusset A)
- Dk homespun - 25 × 10 cm [9⅞" × 4"] (bottom)
- Homespun - 60 × 60 cm [23⅝" × 23⅝"] (backing and inside binding)
- Black homespun - 25 × 15 cm [9⅞" × 6"] (handle loops, tabs)
- Dk homespun - 3.5 × 70 cm [1⅜" × 27½"] (bias binding)
- Batting - 40 × 60 cm [15¾" × 23⅝"]
- Interfacing - 10 × 5 cm [4" × 2"]
- Flannel - 20 × 7 cm [7⅞" × 2¾"]
- 1 zipper - 32 cm [12⅝"]
- Handles - 1 pair
- Embroidery thread - black, grey, dk grey
- Beads - optional (zipper pull)

Instructions

1. Referring to the full-size patterns and the dimensional diagram, cut out all of the pieces of fabric, batting and fusible interfacing for the bag, as well as the appliqué pieces for the design, adding specified seam allowances.

2. Piece together the top (front and back) of the bag; add appliqués and embroidery. Sew the front and back pieces to the bottom piece to create the bag top. Layer the backing and top with batting in between; baste. Quilt as shown or as desired.

3. Make gusset A (zipper opening) by layering both sides with backing and top with batting in between; baste. Quilt. Bind the opening edges (see p. 62) and insert the zipper (diagram 1).

4. Make gusset B (sides) by piecing the various pattern pieces together. Layer the backing and top with batting in between; baste. Quilt as shown or as desired.

5. Make the tabs for each end of the zipper on the gusset (diagram 2).

6. Baste the tabs to each end of gusset A. Sew gusset A and B together (diagram 3).

7. With right sides together and matching seams and edges, pin the quilted bag top and the gusset together. Machine sew, leaving openings (4) where marked for the handle loops to be attached.

8. Make the handle loops (see p. 63) and put them through the handles. Insert the loops into the openings left in step 7 and blindstitch them down on the inside.

9. Make the bias binding and bind the raw seams on the inside.

10. Attach optional zipper pull.

Dimensional Diagram

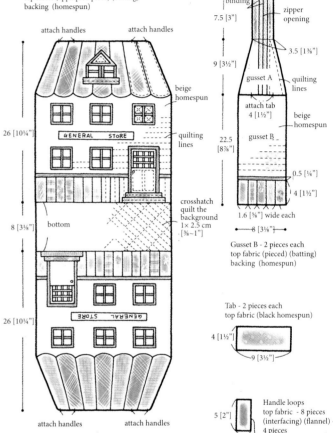

Bag - 1 piece each
top fabric (appliquéd piece) (batting)
backing (homespun)

attach handles attach handles

beige homespun

26 [10¼"]

GENERAL STORE

quilting lines

8 [3⅛"] bottom

crosshatch quilt the background 1 × 2.5 cm [⅜~1"]

26 [10¼"]

GENERAL STORE

attach handles attach handles

22.5 [8⅞"]

Gusset A - 1 piece each
top fabric (dk brown) (batting)
backing (homespun)

center fold

binding

7.5 [3"]

9 [3½"]

zipper opening

3.5 [1⅜"]

gusset A quilting lines

attach tab 4 [1½"]

beige homespun

22.5 [8⅞"]

gusset B

0.5 [¼"]

4 [1½"]

1.6 [⅝"] wide each

8 [3⅛"]

Gusset B - 2 pieces each
top fabric (pieced) (batting)
backing (homespun)

Tab - 2 pieces each
top fabric (black homespun)

4 [1½"]

9 [3½"]

Handle loops
top fabric - 8 pieces
(interfacing) (flannel) - 4 pieces

5 [2"]

2.5 [1"]

Seam allowances: add 0.3-0.5 cm [⅛~¼"] to appliqué; 0.5 cm [¼"] to piecing; 0.7 cm [¼"] to top fabric and flannel; 3 cm [1¼"] to the backing and batting. Cut the interfacing and tabs without any seam allowance.

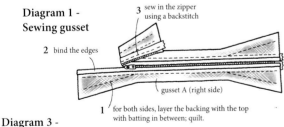

Diagram 1 - Sewing gusset

3 sew in the zipper using a backstitch

2 bind the edges

gusset A (right side)

1 for both sides, layer the backing with the top with batting in between; quilt.

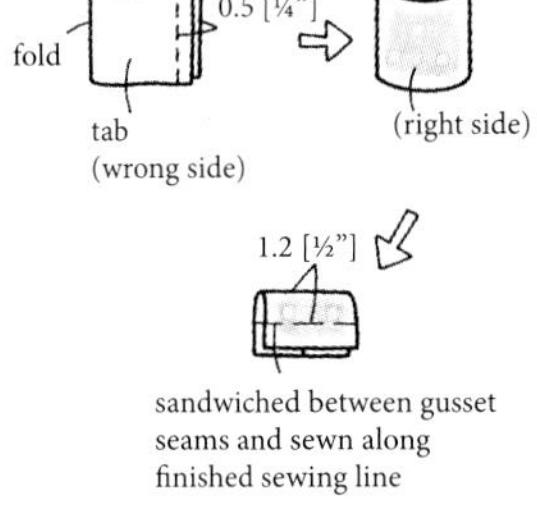

Diagram 3 - Sewing gusset A and B together

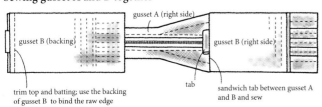

gusset A (right side)

gusset B (backing)

gusset B (right side)

trim top and batting; use the backing of gusset B to bind the raw edge

tab

sandwich tab between gusset A and B and sew

Diagram 2 - Sewing handle loops

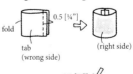

fold

0.5 [¼"]

tab (wrong side)

(right side)

1.2 [½"]

sandwiched between gusset seams and sewn along finished sewing line

Finished Bag

insert the handle loops through the slits at the bottom of the handle. With edges even, insert into the openings in the top of bag at the marks. Blindstitch both on the outside and inside to secure.

GENERAL STORE

Coin Purse: **An Apartment Building** Shown on p. 11

- The full-size template/pattern can be found below.
- Finished measurement: 10 cm [4"] (w) x 15.5 cm [6⅛"] (h); 1 cm [3⅛"] bottom

Materials Needed

Cottons
- Assorted fat quarters or scraps (piecing, appliqué, loops)
- Homespun - 35 × 15 cm [13¾" × 6"] (backing)
- Batting - 35 × 15 cm [13¾" × 6"]
- 1 zipper - 14 cm [5½"]
- Embroidery thread - brown, dk brown, grey
- Beads - optional (zipper pull)
- Leather cord - 10 cm [4"]

Instructions

1. Referring to the template below and the dimensional diagram, with right sides together, cut out 2 background pieces (house shape) adding specified seam allowances. The shapes should mirror each other. Appliqué and embroider the top according to the design.
2. Sew the front and back pieces to the bottom piece to create the coin purse top. Press the seam allowances toward the bottom.
3. Layer the backing and top with right sides together. Place the batting against the backing. Sew around the edges, leaving an opening to turn right side out (diagram 2).
4. Clip corners. Turn right side out; blindstitch the opening closed. Quilt as desired and sew in the zipper (diagram 3).
5. Make the tab (diagram 4). Fold in half and sew it to the bottom where the zipper ends (diagram 5).
6. With right sides together, fold the coin purse in half and sew the edges together with a mattress stitch.

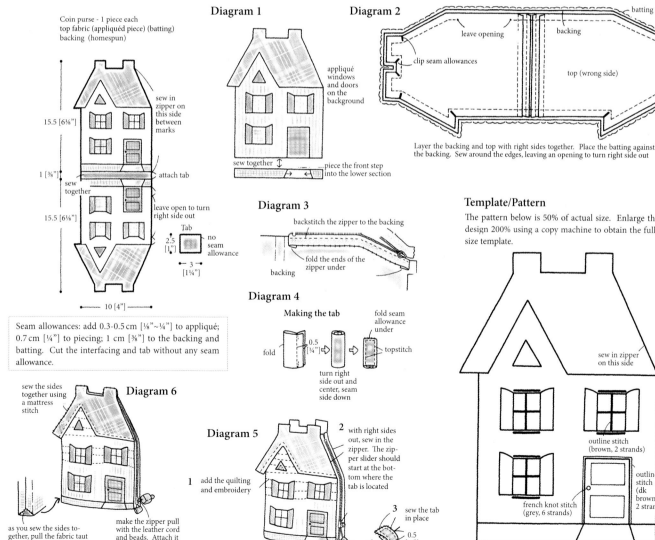

Dimensional Diagram

Coin purse - 1 piece each
top fabric (appliquéd piece) (batting)
backing (homespun)

15.5 [6⅛"]

1 [⅜"]

sew together

15.5 [6⅛"]

sew in zipper on this side between marks

attach tab

leave open to turn right side out

Tab
2.5 [1"]
3 [1¼"]
no seam allowance

10 [4"]

Seam allowances: add 0.3-0.5 cm [⅛"~¼"] to appliqué; 0.7 cm [¼"] to piecing; 1 cm [⅜"] to the backing and batting. Cut the interfacing and tab without any seam allowance.

Diagram 1

appliqué windows and doors on the background

sew together ↕

sew together

piece the front step into the lower section

Diagram 2

batting

leave opening

backing

clip seam allowances

top (wrong side)

Layer the backing and top with right sides together. Place the batting against the backing. Sew around the edges, leaving an opening to turn right side out

Diagram 3

backstitch the zipper to the backing

fold the ends of the zipper under

backing

Diagram 4

Making the tab

fold seam allowance under

fold

0.5 [¼"]

turn right side out and center, seam side down

topstitch

Diagram 6

sew the sides together using a mattress stitch

as you sew the sides together, pull the fabric taut where the bottom meets

make the zipper pull with the leather cord and beads. Attach it to the zipper clasp.

Diagram 5

1 add the quilting and embroidery

2 with right sides out, sew in the zipper. The zipper slider should start at the bottom where the tab is located

3 sew the tab in place

0.5 [¼"]

Template/Pattern

The pattern below is 50% of actual size. Enlarge the design 200% using a copy machine to obtain the full-size template.

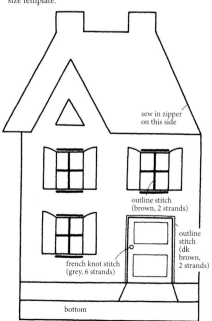

sew in zipper on this side

outline stitch (brown, 2 strands)

outline stitch (dk brown, 2 strands)

french knot stitch (grey, 6 strands)

bottom

Water Bottle Holder: **A Dog at Work, a Cat at Play**   Shown on p. 11

- The full-size template/pattern can be found on Side B of the pattern sheet inserts.
- Finished measurement: 20 cm [7⅞"] (h); 8.2 cm [3¼"] bottom diameter

Materials Needed

Cottons

- Assorted fat quarters or scraps (appliqué)
- Beige homespun - 15 × 30 cm [6" × 11¾"] (top)
- Dk brown homespun - 10 × 10 cm [4" × 4"] (bottom)
- Muslin - 30 × 50 cm [11¾" × 19¾"] (facing)
- Homespun - 8 × 6 cm [3⅛" × 2⅜"] (strap loop)
- Dk homespun - 3.5 × 16 cm [1⅜" × 6¼"] (bias binding)
- Vinyl-coated cotton - 25 × 50 cm [9⅞" × 19¾"] (backing)
- Batting - 30 × 50 cm [11¾" × 19¾"]
- Fusible interfacing - 2 × 3 cm [¾" × 1¼"]
- 1 zipper - 12 cm [4¾"]
- Metal D rings - 2 small
- Embroidery thread - brown, grey, black
- Woven webbing - 22 cm [8⅝"] (strap)
- Waxed cord - 15 cm [6"] optional (zipper pull)

Instructions

1. Referring to the full-size patterns and dimensional diagram, cut out all of the pieces of fabric, batting for the bag, as well as the appliqué pieces for the design, adding specified seam allowances.

2. Appliqué all 3 sides; layer the facing and top with the batting in between; baste. Quilt as desired. Draw the finished sewing lines on the facing.

3. Refer to diagram 1 and with right sides together, sew the quilted pieces to the vinyl-coated cotton. Clip corners and seams where necessary and turn right side out; prick stitch as shown (diagram 2).

4. With right sides together, sew "A" and "C" along the side seam between the marks using a overcast stitch (diagram 3). Insert the zipper (diagram 4). Then with right sides out, sew this piece to "B" along the side seam, using a small overcast stitch, catching only the top fabric and not the vinyl-coated cotton (diagram 5). Measure the diameter of the bottom and make a template. Cut out facing, batting and top fabric for the bottom. Layer them and quilt; draw the finished sewing line on the back. With right sides together, sew the bottom to the backing. Clip and turn right side out and blindstitch the opening (diagram 6).

5. With right sides together, sew the bottom to the sides using a overcast stitch. Turn right side out. Bind the raw edges at the top opening and sew the strap loop in place (diagram 7). Add the optional zipper pull.

Dimensional Diagram

Bag - 1 piece each
top fabric (appliquéd piece) (batting)
facing (muslin)
backing (vinyl)

Strap loop - 1 piece each
top fabric (top)
backing (interfacing)

cut interfacing without seam allowance

Bottom - 1 piece each
top (top) (batting)
facing
backing (vinyl)

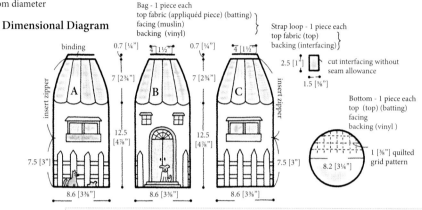

Seam allowances: add 0.3-0.5 cm [⅛"~¼"] to appliqué; 0.7 cm [¼"] to piecing and coated vinyl; 3 cm [1¼"] to the facing and batting. Cut the interfacing and loops without any seam allowance.

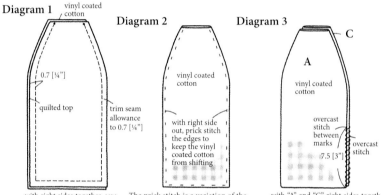

Diagram 1
vinyl coated cotton
0.7 [¼"]
quilted top
trim seam allowance to 0.7 [¼"]
with right sides together, sew the quilted top to the vinyl-coated cotton backing

Diagram 2
vinyl coated cotton
with right side out, prick stitch the edges to keep the vinyl coated cotton from shifting
The prick stitch is a variation of the back stitch. It is mainly used as the hand stitched version of machine understitching, to keep facings/linings from rolling to the outside of the garment.

Diagram 3
C
A
vinyl coated cotton
overcast stitch between marks
overcast stitch
7.5 [3"]
with "A" and "C" right sides together, overcast stitch them together with tiny stitches, catching only the top fabric and not the vinyl-coated cotton backing

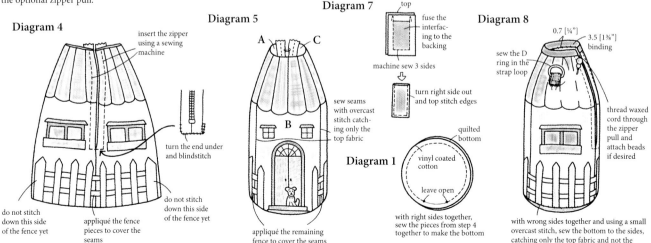

Diagram 4
insert the zipper using a sewing machine
turn the end under and blindstitch
do not stitch down this side of the fence yet
appliqué the fence pieces to cover the seams
do not stitch down this side of the fence yet

Diagram 5
A   C
B
sew seams with overcast stitch catching only the top fabric
appliqué the remaining fence to cover the seams

Diagram 7
top
fuse the interfacing to the backing
machine sew 3 sides
turn right side out and top stitch edges

Diagram 1
quilted bottom
vinyl coated cotton
leave open
with right sides together, sew the pieces from step 4 together to make the bottom

Diagram 8
0.7 [¼"]   3.5 [1⅜"] binding
sew the D ring in the strap loop
thread waxed cord through the zipper pull and attach beads if desired
with wrong sides together and using a small overcast stitch, sew the bottom to the sides, catching only the top fabric and not the vinyl-coated cotton backing

Bag: On My Way Home Shown on p. 12

- The appliqué pattern can be found on Side C of the pattern sheet inserts.
- Finished measurement: 33 cm [13"] (w) × 37cm [14½"] (h)

Materials Needed
Cottons
- Assorted fat quarters or scraps (piecing, appliqué)
- Dk brown print - 40 × 70 cm [15¾" × 27½"] (top)
- Homespun - 43 × 80 cm [16⅞" × 31½"] (backing)
- Homespun - 110 × 40 cm [43¼" × 15¾"] (bias binding)
- Batting - 43 × 80 cm [16⅞" × 31½"]
- Waxed cord - 0.5 cm [¼"] thick × 175 cm [39"] (piping cord)
- Woven webbing - 3 cm [1¼"](w) × 52 cm [20½"] (handles)
- Embroidery thread - black, brown, beige
- Pearl cotton - olive green

Instructions
1. Referring to the appliqué patterns and dimensional diagram, cut out all of the pieces of fabric for the bag, as well as the appliqué pieces for the design, adding specified seam allowances.
2. Add appliqués and embroidery to the front top of the bag. Layer the backing and top with batting in between; baste. Quilt as shown or as desired. Repeat to make the back top of the bag without appliqué. Draw the finished sewing lines on the top of both quilted pieces.
3. Measure around the sides and bottom of the bag as well as the top opening + 10 cm [4"] and make a 2.5 cm [1"] bias strip to that length. Using the waxed cord, make piping cord (see diagram 1). Position it on the front top of the bag (diagram 2) and baste in place. Then, with right sides together, pin the front top and back top in place. Machine sew around the edge, making sure to sew along the edge of the piping cord.
4. Trim the front top and batting to 0.7 cm [¼"]. Bind the inside seam allowance with the backing fabric and blindstitch down to the backing.
5. With right sides together, layer the piping cord, handle and a 3 cm [1¼"] bias strip (length = perimeter of the opening) and sew on the finished sewing line. Fold the bias binding over and use to bind the raw edges around the opening.

Dimensional Diagram

Front Bag - 1 piece each
top fabric (appliquéd piece) (batting)
backing (homespun)

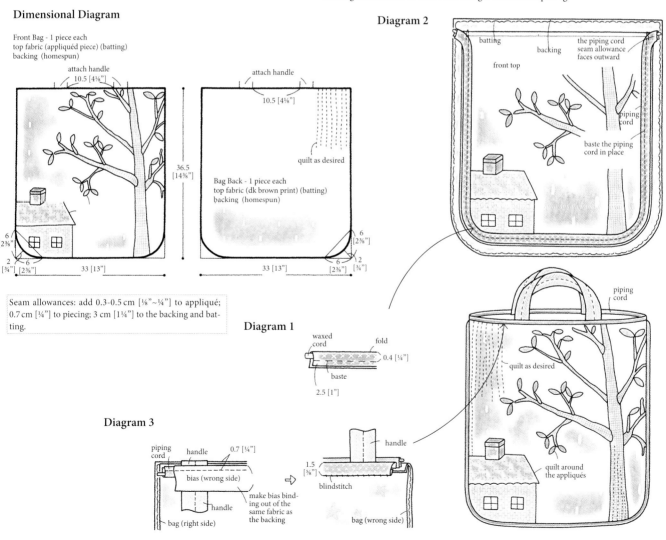

Seam allowances: add 0.3-0.5 cm [⅛"~¼"] to appliqué; 0.7 cm [¼"] to piecing; 3 cm [1¼"] to the backing and batting.

Bucket Bag: **Going Uphill, 'Round and 'Round**   Shown on p. 13

- The full-size template/pattern can be found on Side B of the pattern sheet inserts.
- Finished measurement: 21 cm [8¼"] (h); 18.4 cm [7¼"] bottom diameter

Materials Needed

Cottons

- Assorted fat quarters or scraps (appliqué)
- Brown homespun - 65 × 35 cm [25½" × 13¾"] (top)
- Dk brown homespun - 50 × 30 cm [19¾" × 11¾"] (bottom, piping cord)
- Plaid homespun - 85 × 30 cm [33½" × 11¾"] (lining)
- Muslin - 85 × 30 cm [33½" × 11¾"] (facing)
- Batting - 85 × 30 cm [33½" × 11¾"]
- Fusible interfacing - 75 × 30 cm [29½" × 11¾"]
- Leather handle - 1.8-2.7 cm [¾"~1"] × 31 cm [12¼"]
- Waxed cord - 0.3 cm [⅛"] thick × 50 cm [19¾"] (for piping cord)
- Embroidery thread - black, grey

Instructions

1. Referring to the full-size patterns and dimensional diagram, cut out all of the pieces of fabric, batting for the bag, as well as the appliqué pieces for the design, adding specified seam allowances.
2. Appliqué the top 3 slanting fabric pieces of the bag and then sew them together. Add the embroidered stars and rays onto the top. Then layer the facing and top with the batting in between; baste. Quilt as desired.
3. With right sides together, fold the bag so that the side seam is aligned and sew. Press the seam open.
4. Measure around the top opening + 5cm [2"] and make a 2.5 cm [1"] bias strip to that length. Using the waxed cord, make piping cord (see diagram 1). Position it on the top of the bag with right sides together, as shown, and baste in place. Machine sew.
5. Fuse the interfacing to the wrong side of the lining and with right sides together, sew the side seam and press it open.
6. With right sides together, align the raw edges of the top and the lining at the opening and sew around the edge making sure to sew along the edge of the piping cord. Turn the piece right side out and flip the lining to the inside. Smooth down and baste the bottom raw edges together to hold the lining in place.
7. Next, layer the top fabric of the bottom of the bag with the facing with the batting in between; machine quilt as shown.
8. Turn the bag (cylinder) with the lining facing out and pin the bottom to it, with right sides together, and sew.
9. Prepare the inner bottom lining (diagram 2) and blindstitch to the lining covering the raw edges. Turn right side out.
10. Make the handle loops and slip through the leather handle; sew them to the inside of the bag (diagram 3).

Dimensional Diagram

Bag - 1 piece each
top fabric (appliquéd piece)
Facing (muslin) and (batting)
lining (plaid homespun)

Handle loop - 1 piece each
top fabric (top) (backing)
scrap (batting) (interfacing)

cut interfacing without seam allowance

3 [1¼"]
2 [¾"]

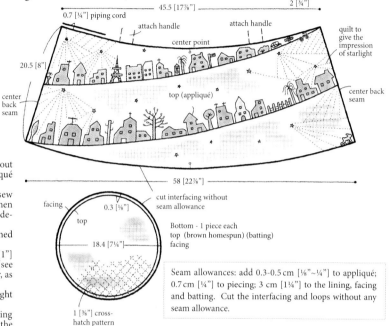

0.7 [¼"] piping cord
attach handle
attach handle
center point
quilt to give the impression of starlight
45.5 [17⅞"]
20.5 [8"]
center back seam
top (appliqué)
center back seam
58 [22⅞"]

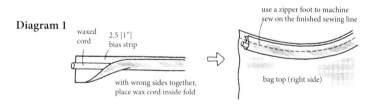

cut interfacing without seam allowance
facing
0.3 [⅛"]
top
18.4 [7¼"]
1 [⅜"] cross-hatch pattern

Bottom - 1 piece each
top (brown homespun) (batting)
facing

Seam allowances: add 0.3-0.5 cm [⅛"~¼"] to appliqué; 0.7 cm [¼"] to piecing; 3 cm [1¼"] to the lining, facing and batting. Cut the interfacing and loops without any seam allowance.

Diagram 1

waxed cord
2.5 [1"] bias strip
with wrong sides together, place wax cord inside fold

use a zipper foot to machine sew on the finished sewing line
bag top (right side)

Diagram 2

finished bag

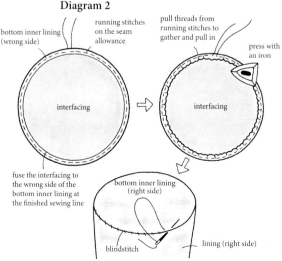

bottom inner lining (wrong side)
running stitches on the seam allowance
pull threads from running stitches to gather and pull in
press with an iron
interfacing
interfacing
fuse the interfacing to the wrong side of the bottom inner lining at the finished sewing line
bottom inner lining (right side)
blindstitch
lining (right side)

Diagram 3

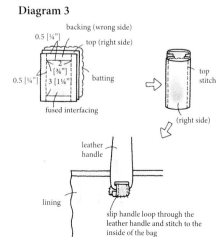

backing (wrong side)
top (right side)
0.5 [¼"]
2 [¾"]
0.5 [¼"]
3 [1¼"]
batting
fused interfacing
top stitch
(right side)
leather handle
lining
slip handle loop through the leather handle and stitch to the inside of the bag

Handbag: **The View of a Chimney Sweep** Shown on p. 15

- The full-size template/pattern can be found on Side B of the pattern sheet inserts.
- Finished measurement: 14 cm [5½"] (h) × 29 cm [11⅜"] (w); 8 cm [3⅛"] gusset

Materials Needed

Cottons
- Assorted scraps (windows - appliqué)
- Striped homespun - 40 × 45 cm [15¾" × 17⅝"] (top, gusset A and B)
- Dk homespun - 110 × 20 cm [43¼" × 7⅞"] (buildings - appliqué, gusset B)
- Homespun - 9 × 12 cm [3½" × 4¾"] (tabs)
- Homespun - 110 × 30 cm [43¼" × 11¾"] (backing)
- Striped homespun - 3.5 × 36 cm [1⅜" × 14⅛"] (binding for gusset A)
- Batting - 110 × 30 cm [43¼" × 11¾"]
- Fusible interfacing - 8 × 45 cm [3⅛" × 17⅝"]
- 1 zipper - 33 cm [13"]
- 2 leather handles - 1.5 cm [⅝"] × 33 cm [13"]
- Embroidery thread - black, grey, dk beige
- Bead - optional (zipper pull)
- Waxed cord - 10 cm [4"] optional (zipper pull)

Instructions

1. Referring to the appliqué patterns and dimensional diagram, cut out all of the pieces of fabric and batting for the bag, as well as the appliqué pieces for the design, adding specified seam allowances.

2. Use the reverse appliqué technique (p. 56) to appliqué the windows to the buildings. Then add building appliqué and embroidery to the front top of the bag. Layer the backing and top with batting in between; baste. Quilt as shown or as desired. Repeat to make the back top of the bag.

3. Make gusset A (zipper opening) by layering both sides with backing and top with batting in between; baste. Quilt. Bind the opening edges (see p. 62) and insert the zipper (diagram 2).

4. Make gusset B (sides and bottom) by piecing the dk and striped homespuns together. Fuse the interfacing to the wrong side. Layer the fused backing and top with batting in between; baste. Quilt as shown or as desired.

5. Make the tabs for each end of the zipper on the gusset (diagram 1).

6. Baste the tabs to each end of gusset A. Sew gusset A and B together (diagram 2); trim seam allowance of the top and batting and use the backing to bind the raw edges. With right sides together, sew the gusset B pieces together making the center bottom seam (diagram 3).

7. Baste the handles to the right side of the bag. With right sides together and matching seams and edges, pin the quilted bag top and the gusset together and trim top and batting.

8. Starting on the gusset, bind the raw seam allowance on both sides of the bag using a blindstitch using the backing. Turn the bag right side out to complete (diagram 4).

Dimensional Diagram

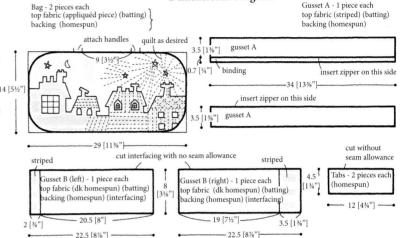

Bag - 2 pieces each
top fabric (appliquéd piece) (batting)
backing (homespun)

attach handles · quilt as desired

9 [3½"]

14 [5½"]

29 [11⅜"]

cut interfacing with no seam allowance

striped

Gusset A - 1 piece each
top fabric (striped) (batting)
backing (homespun)

3.5 [1⅜"] gusset A

0.7 [¼"] binding

34 [13⅜"]

insert zipper on this side

insert zipper on this side

3.5 [1⅜"] gusset A

cut without seam allowance

striped

Gusset B (left) - 1 piece each
top fabric (dk homespun) (batting)
backing (homespun) (interfacing)

Gusset B (right) - 1 piece each
top fabric (dk homespun) (batting)
backing (homespun) (interfacing)

Tabs - 2 pieces each
(homespun)

8 [3⅛"]

4.5 [1¾"]

2 [¾"]   20.5 [8"]   19 [7½"]   3.5 [1⅜"]

22.5 [8⅞"]   22.5 [8⅞"]   12 [4¾"]

Seam allowances: add 0.3-0.5 cm [⅛"~¼"] to upper edge of appliqué; 1 cm [⅜"] to lower and side edges of appliqué; 0.7 cm [¼"] to piecing; 3 cm [1¼"] to the lining, facing and batting. Cut the interfacing and tabs without any seam allowance.

Diagram 1

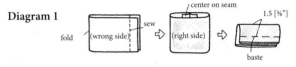

fold   (wrong side)   sew   center on seam   (right side)   1.5 [⅝"]   baste

Diagram 2

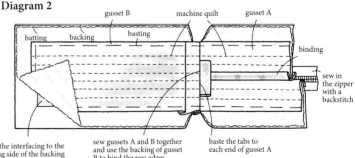

gusset B   machine quilt   gusset A

batting   backing   basting   binding

sew in the zipper with a backstitch

fuse the interfacing to the wrong side of the backing (cut without seam allowance for the interfacing)

sew gussets A and B together and use the backing of gusset B to bind the raw edges

baste the tabs to each end of gusset A

Diagram 3

basting

with right sides together, sew gusset B pieces together to make a cylinder shape; trim the top and batting; bind the raw edges with the backing fabric.

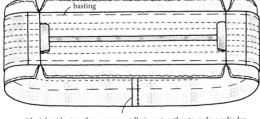

Diagram 4

make the zipper pull with the waxed cord and bead; attach it to the zipper clasp

baste the handles to the right side of the bag before sewing the gusset to the bag top and back

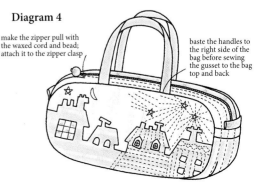

Backpack: **Antennas** Shown on p. 14

- The full-size template/pattern can be found on Side B of the pattern sheet inserts.
- Finished measurement: 18 cm [7⅛"] (w) × 24 cm [9⅜"] (h); 5 cm [2"] gusset

Materials Needed

Cottons

- 20 assorted fat quarters or scraps (appliqué)
- Plaid homespun - 70 × 55 cm [27½" × 21⅝"] (top, gusset A, B, pocket, pocket gusset, bias binding for the inside of pocket)
- Homespun - 70 × 80 cm [27½" × 31½"] (backing, partition, bias binding for the inside of bag)
- Homespun - 30 × 30 cm [11¾" × 11¾"] (bias binding for gusset, strap joint loops)
- Dk homespun - 3.5 × 20 cm [1⅜" × 7⅞"] - 2 pieces (bias binding for the front of bag and pocket)

- Batting - 40 × 110 cm [15¾" × 43¼"]
- Fusible interfacing - 35 × 60 cm [13¾" × 123⅝"]
- 3 zippers - 16 cm [6¼"]; 17cm [6⅝"]; 30 cm [11¾"]
- Metal hardward - 2 rectangle rings; 1 double ring (width of strap)
- Woven webbing - 3 cm [1¼"] (w) × 150 cm [59⅛"] (strap)
- Waxed cord - 15 cm [6"] optional (zipper pull)
- Beads - optional (zipper pull)
- Embroidery thread - black

Seam allowances: add 0.3-0.5 cm [⅛"~¼"] to appliqué; 0.7 cm [¼"] to piecing; 3 cm [1¼"] to the backing and batting. Cut the interfacing without any seam allowance.

Instructions

1. Referring to the full-size patterns and dimensional diagram, cut out all of the pieces of fabric, batting for the bag, as well as the appliqué pieces for the design, adding specified seam allowances.
2. Appliqué the front pocket (lower section) and add embroidery. Layer the pocket top and backing with batting in between; baste. Quilt as desired. Then, layer the top and backing with batting in between for the upper pocket section; baste. Quilt as desired. Use the 3.5 [1⅜"] dark homespun bias binding to bind the raw seam allowance.
3. Insert the zipper between the upper and lower pocket sections (diagram 1).
4. Make the gusset for the pocket and with right sides together, sew it to the front pocket from step 2. Make a 2.5 cm [1"] bias binding from the plaid homespun and bind the inside raw edges (diagram 2).
5. Make 3 separate quilted pieces for the upper and lower sections of the main bag and the bag back. Quilt each as shown or as desired. Use more of the 3.5 [1⅜"] dark homespun bias binding to bind the raw seam allowance on the upper section (as was done for the pocket). Insert the zipper between the upper and lower sections of the main bag.
6. Cut 2 partition pieces. Create a partition for the upper zipper on the main bag by fusing interfacing to the wrong size of one piece and then with wrong sides together and the interfacing in between, baste them together around the edge. Place the main bag front on top of the partition piece, pin in place and machine stitch 0.5 cm [¼"] around the edge (diagram 3).
7. Make 3 separate quilted pieces for the main bag gusset (on either side of the zipper and around the bag). Sew the zipper between the 2 gusset A pieces. Make 2 strap joint loops and insert through the metal rectangle rings. Baste the strap joint loops with rings to each end of the gusset A (zipper). With right sides together, sew gusset B on each end to gusset A (diagram 4).
8. With right sides together, sew the main bag gusset to the main bag top. Use a 2.5 cm [1"] bias binding from the plaid homespun and bind the inside raw edges. Repeat this to sew the gusset to the main bag back.
9. Blindstitch the front pocket onto the surface of the main bag front.
10. To attach the shoulder strap, put the woven webbing through the rectangle ring on the right and sew it in place with the raw edge on the inside. Next, feed the woven webbing through the double ring (above the bar slide) and then through the rectangle ring on the left, from the outside in toward the bag. Pull it up toward the double ring and fold the raw end over the middle bar and back (approximately 2-2.5 cm [¾"~1"]) and sew in place to secure (see close up in finished bag diagram). Attach beads to the zipper clasp using the waxed cord if desired.

Dimensional Diagram

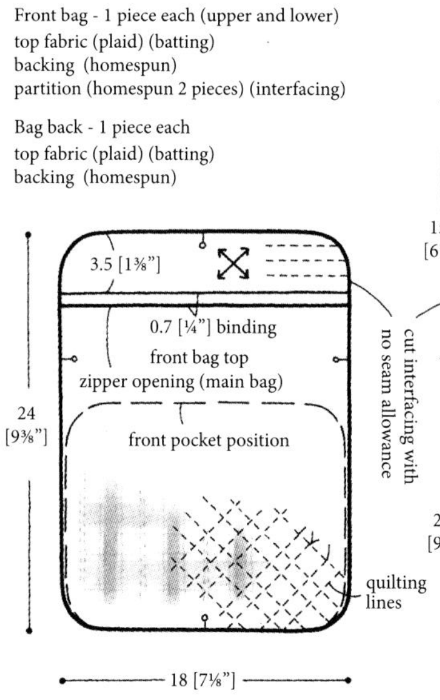

Front bag - 1 piece each (upper and lower)
top fabric (plaid) (batting)
backing (homespun)
partition (homespun 2 pieces) (interfacing)
Bag back - 1 piece each
top fabric (plaid) (batting)
backing (homespun)
3.5 [1⅜"]
0.7 [¼"] binding
front bag top
zipper opening (main bag)
front pocket position
24 [9⅜"]
quilting lines
18 [7⅛"]
cut interfacing with no seam allowance

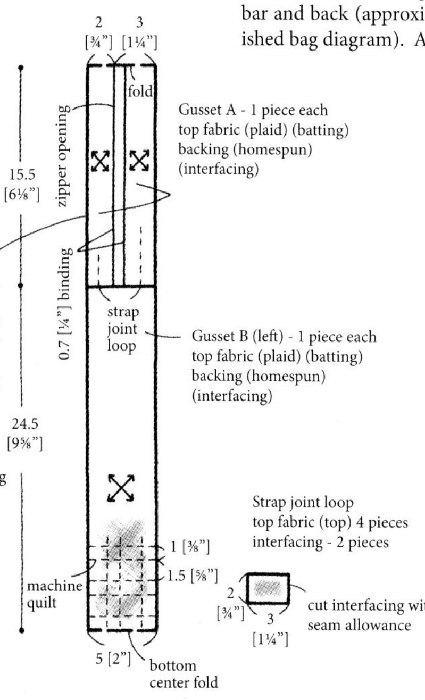

2 [¾"]
3 [1¼"]
fold
zipper opening
15.5 [6⅛"]
Gusset A - 1 piece each
top fabric (plaid) (batting)
backing (homespun)
(interfacing)
0.7 [¼"] binding
strap joint loop
Gusset B (left) - 1 piece each
top fabric (plaid) (batting)
backing (homespun)
(interfacing)
24.5 [9⅝"]
1 [⅜"]
1.5 [⅝"]
machine quilt
5 [2"]
bottom center fold
Strap joint loop
top fabric (top) 4 pieces
interfacing - 2 pieces
2 [¾"]
3 [1¼"]
cut interfacing without seam allowance

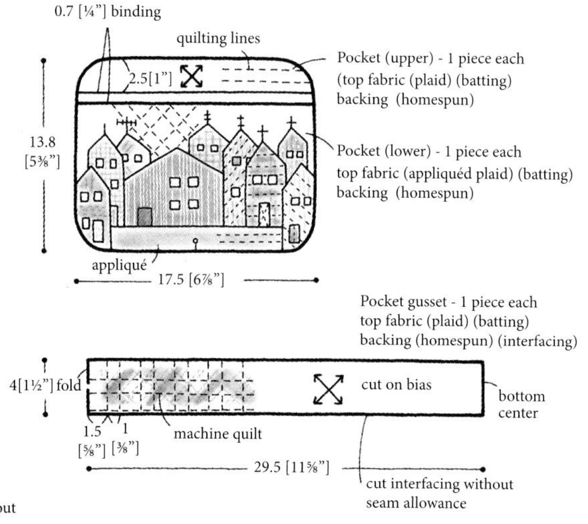

0.7 [¼"] binding
quilting lines
2.5[1"]
Pocket (upper) - 1 piece each
(top fabric (plaid) (batting)
backing (homespun)
13.8 [5⅜"]
Pocket (lower) - 1 piece each
top fabric (appliquéd plaid) (batting)
backing (homespun)
appliqué
17.5 [6⅞"]
Pocket gusset - 1 piece each
top fabric (plaid) (batting)
backing (homespun) (interfacing)
4[1½"] fold
cut on bias
bottom center
1.5 [⅝"]
1 [⅜"]
machine quilt
29.5 [11⅝"]
cut interfacing without seam allowance

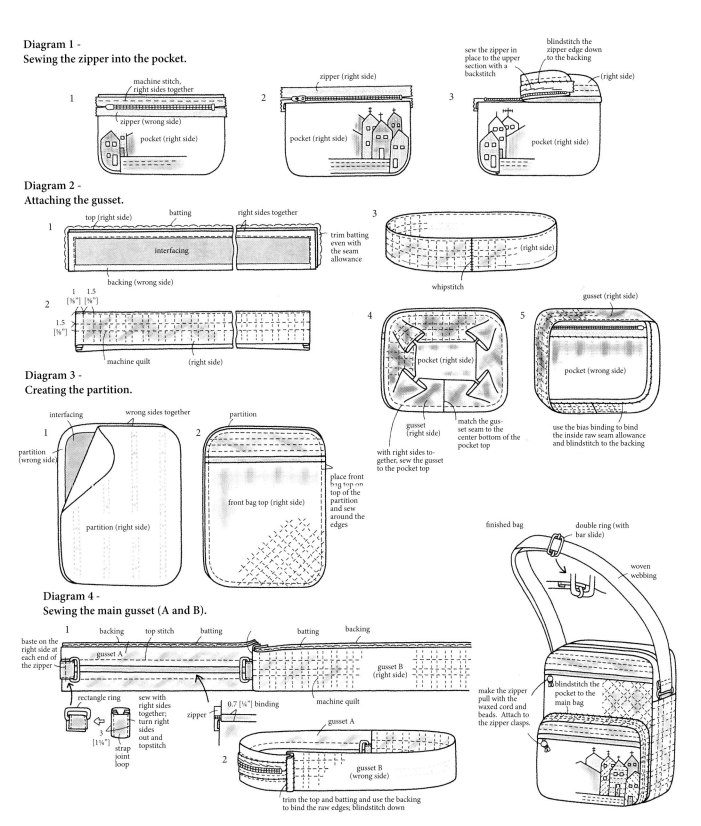

Diagram 1 -
Sewing the zipper into the pocket.

1 machine stitch, right sides together
zipper (wrong side)
pocket (right side)

2 zipper (right side)
pocket (right side)

3 sew the zipper in place to the upper section with a backstitch
blindstitch the zipper edge down to the backing
(right side)
pocket (right side)

Diagram 2 -
Attaching the gusset.

1 top (right side) batting right sides together
interfacing
backing (wrong side)
trim batting even with the seam allowance

2 1 [⅜"] 1.5 [⅝"]
1.5 [⅝"]
machine quilt (right side)

3 (right side)
whipstitch

4 pocket (right side)
gusset (right side)
match the gusset seam to the center bottom of the pocket top
with right sides together, sew the gusset to the pocket top

5 gusset (right side)
pocket (wrong side)
use the bias binding to bind the inside raw seam allowance and blindstitch to the backing

Diagram 3 -
Creating the partition.

1 interfacing wrong sides together
partition (wrong side)
partition (right side)

2 partition
front bag top (right side)
place front bag top on top of the partition and sew around the edges

finished bag
double ring (with bar slide)
woven webbing
blindstitch the pocket to the main bag

Diagram 4 -
Sewing the main gusset (A and B).

1 baste on the right side at each end of the zipper
backing top stitch batting
gusset A
batting backing
gusset B (right side)
machine quilt
rectangle ring
sew with right sides together; turn right sides out and topstitch
3 [1¼"]
strap joint loop
zipper
0.7 [¼"] binding
make the zipper pull with the waxed cord and beads. Attach to the zipper clasps.

2 gusset A
gusset B (wrong side)
trim the top and batting and use the backing to bind the raw edges; blindstitch down

Bag: **Japanese Houses**   Shown on p. 16

- The full-size template/pattern can be found on Side B of the pattern sheet inserts.
- Finished measurement: 32 cm [12⅝"] (w) × 38 cm [15"] (h); 10 cm [4"] gusset

Materials Needed
Cottons
- Assorted fat quarters or scraps (appliqué)
- Homespun A - 10 × 70 cm [4" × 27½"] (A)
- Homespun B - 10 × 70 cm [4" × 27½"] (B)
- Corduroy - 20 × 55 cm [7⅞" × 21⅝"] (C, top fabric for bag bottom, handle loops)
- Homespun D - 25 × 70 cm [9⅞" × 27½"] (D)
- Homespun - 110 × 50 cm [43¼" × 19¾"] (backing, bias binding for opening)
- Batting - 60 × 60 cm [23⅝" × 23⅝"]
- Fusible interfacing - 10 × 35 cm [4" × 13¾"]
- Embroidery thread - black, brown
- Handles - 1 pair

Instructions
1. Referring to the appliqué patterns and dimensional diagram, cut out all of the pieces of fabric and batting for the bag, as well as the appliqué pieces for the design, adding specified seam allowances.
2. Add appliqués and embroidery to piece "B". Sew piece "C" to the bottom of "B".
3. Sew piece "A" to the top edge of "B" and piece "D" to the bottom of "C" to complete the bag top. Layer the top and backing with the batting in between; baste. Quilt around the appliqués and inside each house. Quilt the background of piece "B" to give the impression of wind currents. Repeat steps 2 and 3 to create the back side of the bag.
4. Refer to diagram 1 to make the bottom of the bag. Then, with right sides together, sew the bottom to the front and back of the bag, matching the edges. Trim the top and batting, leaving the backing to bind the raw seam allowances on the inside of the bag, using a blindstitch to sew down to the backing (diagram 2).
5. Refer to diagram 3 and p. 69 to sew the bag bottom to the side seams.
6. Make the handle loops (diagram 4); slip through handles and baste loop ends together.
7. Baste the handles to the right side of the bag opening. Make a 3 cm [1¼"] bias binding (length = perimeter of the opening). With right sides together, align the binding and bag opening edge and sew on the finished sewing line, catching the handle loops in the stitching. Fold the binding over and use it to bind the raw edges around the inside opening.

Dimensional Diagram

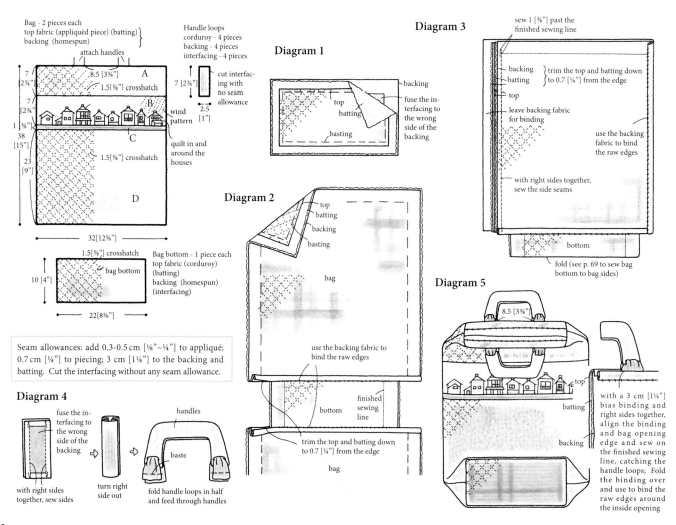

Seam allowances: add 0.3-0.5 cm [⅛"~¼"] to appliqué; 0.7 cm [¼"] to piecing; 3 cm [1¼"] to the backing and batting. Cut the interfacing without any seam allowance.

Handbag: **Windmills** *Shown on p. 17*

- The full-size template/pattern can be found on Side C of the pattern sheet inserts.
- Finished measurement: 27 cm [10⅝"] (h); 34 cm [13⅜"] (opening width)

Materials Needed
Cottons
- 28 assorted fat quarters or scraps (appliqué)
- 2 ecru print - 40 ×30 cm [15¾"×11¾"] each (top - print A, B)
- Homespun - 110×70 cm [43¼"×27½"] (backing)
- Plaid homespun - 55 ×30 cm [21⅝"×11¾"] (opening, bias binding for opening, top fabric for bottom)
- Print - 30 ×30 cm [11¾"×11¾"] (pleat - top)
- Homespun - 50 ×50 cm [19¾"×19¾"] (bias binding)
- Batting - 60 ×60 cm [23⅝"×23⅝"]
- Fusible interfacing - 45 ×35 cm [17⅝"×13¾"]
- Woven webbing - 30 cm [11¾"] 2 pieces (handles)
- Embroidery thread - black, grey, dk grey, dk brown

Instructions
1. Referring to the full-size patterns and dimensional diagram, cut out all of the pieces of fabric, batting for the bag, as well as the appliqué pieces for the design, adding specified seam allowances.
2. Add appliqués and embroidery to the top piece of the bag. Layer the backing and top with batting in between; baste. Quilt as shown or as desired. Repeat to make all 4 top pieces.
3. Attach the pleat fabric to the top pieces (diagram 1).
4. Sew the opening fabric to the top of the bag; quilt. Baste handles in place, then sew bias binding to the opening of the bag (diagram 2).
5. Sew the two bag sections (front and back) together at the side seams with wrong sides together. Trim seam allowance to 0.7 cm [¼"]. Make a 3.5 cm [1⅜"] wide bias binding (length = bag side seams + 10 cm [4"]). Bind the 2 side seams.
6. Fuse the interfacing to the bottom backing fabric; layer with top fabric for bottom with batting in between; machine quilt.
7. With wrong sides together, sew the bag to the bottom. Trim seam allowance to 0.7 cm [¼"]. Use a 3.5 cm [1⅜"] wide bias binding (length = bottom perimeter + 10 cm [4"]). Bind the raw seams around the bottom.

Diagram 1 - Putting in the Pleats

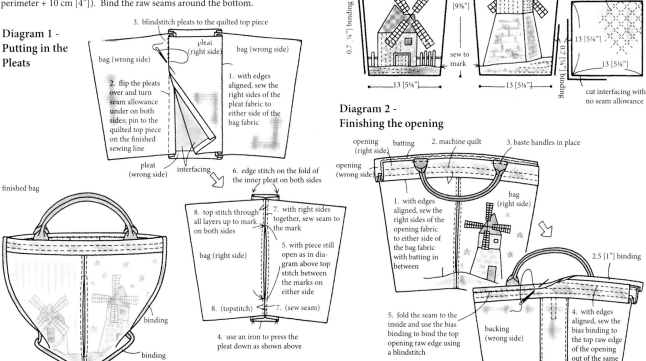

finished bag

3. blindstitch pleats to the quilted top piece

pleat (right side)

bag (wrong side)

bag (wrong side)

1. with edges aligned, sew the right sides of the pleat fabric to either side of the bag fabric

2. flip the pleats over and turn seam allowance under on both sides; pin to the quilted top piece on the finished sewing line

pleat (wrong side)   interfacing

6. edge stitch on the fold of the inner pleat on both sides

8. top stitch through all layers up to mark on both sides

7. with right sides together, sew seam to the mark

bag (right side)

5. with piece still open as in diagram above top stitch between the marks on either side

8. (topstitch)   7. (sew seam)

4. use an iron to press the pleat down as shown above

binding
binding
binding

Dimensional Diagram

Seam allowances: add 0.3-0.5 cm [⅛"~¼"] to appliqué; 0.7 cm [¼"] to piecing; 3 cm [1¼"] to the backing and batting. Cut the interfacing and loops without any seam allowance.

Opening
top fabric (plaid) - 4 pieces each
(batting) (homespun) - 2 pieces each

attach handles   16 [6¼"]   attach handles

3 [1¼"]   cut on bias   machine quilt

34 [13⅜"]

cut interfacing with no seam allowance

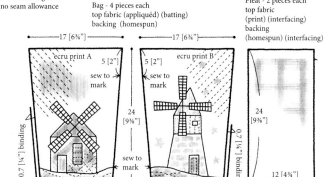

Bag - 4 pieces each
top fabric (appliquéd) (batting)
backing (homespun)

17 [6¾"]   17 [6¾"]

ecru print A   5 [2"]   5 [2"]   ecru print B

sew to mark   sew to mark

24 [9⅜"]

0.7 [¼"] binding   0.7 [¼"] binding

sew to mark

13 [5⅝"]   13 [5⅝"]

Pleat - 2 pieces each
top fabric
(print) (interfacing)
backing
(homespun) (interfacing)

24 [9⅜"]

12 [4¾"]

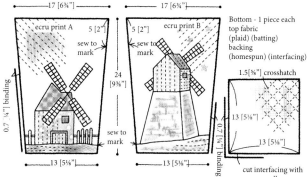

17 [6¾"]   17 [6¾"]

ecru print A   5 [2"]   5 [2"]   ecru print B

sew to mark   sew to mark

24 [9⅜"]

0.7 [¼"] binding   0.7 [¼"] binding

sew to mark

13 [5⅛"]   13 [5⅛"]

Bottom - 1 piece each
top fabric
(plaid) (batting)
backing
(homespun) (interfacing)

1.5 [⅝"] crosshatch

13 [5⅛"]

13 [5⅛"]

cut interfacing with no seam allowance

Diagram 2 - Finishing the opening

opening (right side)   batting   2. machine quilt   3. baste handles in place

opening (wrong side)

1. with edges aligned, sew the right sides of the opening fabric to either side of the bag fabric with batting in between

bag (right side)

2.5 [1"] binding

5. fold the seam to the inside and use the bias binding to bind the top opening raw edge using a blindstitch

backing (wrong side)

4. with edges aligned, sew the bias binding to the top raw edge of the opening out of the same plaid fabric

93

Pouch: **Linus's Little Red House**   Shown on p. 20

- The full-size template/pattern can be found on Side C of the pattern sheet inserts.
- Finished measurement: 11 cm [4⅜"] (w) × 14 cm [5½"] (h); 3 cm [1¼"] gusset

Materials Needed

Cottons
- Assorted fat quarters or scraps (piecing, appliqué, tab loops)
- Homespun - 12 × 10 cm [4¾"× 4"] (gusset)
- Print - 36 × 25 cm [14⅛"× 9⅞"] (backing, inside binding)
- Homespun - 2.5 × 80 cm [1"× 31½"] (bias binding)
- Batting - 36 × 25 cm [14⅛"× 9⅞"]
- 1 zipper - 16 cm [6¼"]
- Waxed cord - 0.3 cm [⅛"] thick × 80 cm [31½"]
- Embroidery thread - black, grey
- Beads - optional (zipper pull)
- Leather cord - 10 cm [4"] (brown)

Instructions

1. Referring to the template/pattern and the dimensional diagram, piece, appliqué and embroider to make the front and back sections, adding specified seam allowances. Sew the front and back piece to the bottom piece to create the pouch top. Press the seam allowances toward the bottom.
2. Layer the backing and top with batting in between; baste. Quilt as desired.
3. Make the piping cord from the bias binding and waxed cord (diagram 1). Baste it around the edges of the front and back piece as shown (diagram 2).
4. Make the tab loops (diagram 3) and baste to the end of the zipper. Make the gusset by sewing the zipper ends sandwiched between the quilted gusset pieces (diagram 4). Make sure to catch the loops in the seam.
5. With right sides together, sew the bag and zipper/gusset to each other, centering the zipper on the top and the gusset seam at the bottom. Using the same fabric as the backing, make a 2.5 [1"] wide bias binding and bind the inside raw edges of the pouch.
6. String the beads on the leather cord and tie together to the zipper clasp (optional).

Dimensional Diagram

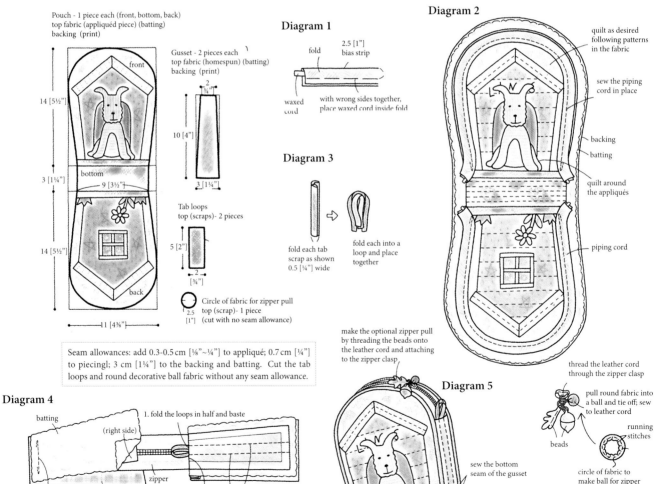

Pouch - 1 piece each (front, bottom, back)
top fabric (appliquéd piece) (batting)
backing (print)

front

14 [5½"]

bottom

9 [3½"]

3 [1¼"]

14 [5½"]

back

11 [4⅜"]

Gusset - 2 pieces each
top fabric (homespun) (batting)
backing (print)

2 [¾"]

10 [4"]

3 [1¼"]

Tab loops
top (scraps)- 2 pieces

5 [2"]

2 [¾"]

Circle of fabric for zipper pull
top (scrap)- 1 piece
(cut with no seam allowance)
2.5 [1"]

Seam allowances: add 0.3-0.5 cm [⅛"~¼"] to appliqué; 0.7 cm [¼"] to piecingl; 3 cm [1¼"] to the backing and batting. Cut the tab loops and round decorative ball fabric without any seam allowance.

Diagram 1

fold

2.5 [1"]
bias strip

waxed cord

with wrong sides together, place waxed cord inside fold

Diagram 2

quilt as desired following patterns in the fabric

sew the piping cord in place

backing

batting

quilt around the appliqués

piping cord

Diagram 3

fold each tab scrap as shown 0.5 [¼"] wide

fold each into a loop and place together

make the optional zipper pull by threading the beads onto the leather cord and attaching to the zipper clasp

thread the leather cord through the zipper clasp

pull round fabric into a ball and tie off; sew to leather cord

running stitches

beads

circle of fabric to make ball for zipper pull

Diagram 4

batting

(right side)

1. fold the loops in half and baste

zipper

(wrong side)

2. sandwich the zipper ends between the gusset and batting and sew seams

3. Turn gusset right side out

4. quilt both sides of the gusset

Diagram 5

sew the bottom seam of the gusset

sew the gusset, zipper and bag together

Pouch: **Birdhouses** Shown on p. 21

- The full-size template/pattern can be found on Side B of the pattern sheet inserts.
- Finished measurement: 20 cm [7⅞"] (w) × 10-11 cm [4~4⅜"] (h); 6 cm [2⅜"] gusset

Materials Needed

Cottons

- Assorted fat quarters or scraps (appliqué, zipper fabric tabs)
- Print - 11 × 45 cm [4⅜" × 17¾"] (top)
- Homespun - 20 × 20 cm [7⅞" × 7⅞"] (bottom)
- Homespun - 20 × 20 cm [7⅞" × 7⅞"] (gusset top fabric)
- Homespun - 30 × 40 cm [11¾" × 15¾"] (backing)
- Homespun - 3.5 × 90 cm [1⅜" × 35⅜"] (bias binding)
- Fusible interfacing - 10 × 15 cm [4" × 6"]
- Batting - 30 × 40 cm [11¾" × 15¾"]
- 1 zipper - 22.5 cm [8⅞"]
- Beads - optional (zipper pull)
- Leather cord - 15 cm [6"] (moss green)

Instructions

1. Referring to the template/pattern and the dimensional diagram, piece and appliqué the birdhouses to the top fabric to make the front and back sections, adding specified seam allowances.

2. Sew the front and back piece to the bottom piece to create the top. Press the seam allowances toward the bottom. Layer the backing and top with batting in between; baste. Quilt as desired.

3. Refer to diagram 2 to make the gusset. With wrong sides together and edges matching, pin the gusset to the bag; machine sew around the edges (diagram 3).

4. Sew the zipper fabric tab onto the end of the zipper (diagram 4). Sew the zipper tape to the bag opening, aligning the tape to the top of the opening on each side (diagram 5).

5. Make 3.5 cm [1¼"] wide bias binding and pin, with right sides together, to the outside of the pouch. Sew on the finished sewing lines. Fold the binding toward the zipper/gusset and blindstitch down.

6. Thread the leather cord through the zipper clasp, add beads and knot to make a zipper pull (optional).

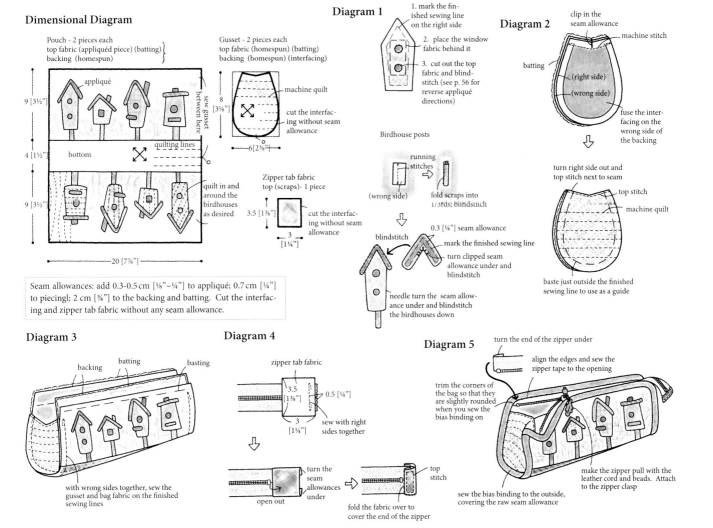

Seam allowances: add 0.3-0.5 cm [⅛"~¼"] to appliqué; 0.7 cm [¼"] to piecingl; 2 cm [¾"] to the backing and batting. Cut the interfacing and zipper tab fabric without any seam allowance.

Coin Purse: **A Bike Parked on a Corner** Shown on p. 22

- The full-size template/pattern can be found on Side C of the pattern sheet inserts.
- Finished measurement: 13 cm [5⅛"] (w) x 11.5 cm [4½"] (h); 1.8 cm [¾"] gusset

Materials Needed
Cottons
- Assorted fat quarters or scraps (piecing, appliqué, bottom)
- Homespun - 27 x 16 cm [10⅝" x 6¼"] (backing)
- Batting - 27 x 16 cm [10⅝" x 6¼"]
- Fusible interfacing - 1.5 x 26 cm [⅝" x 10¼"]
- 1 purse squeeze frame - 1.7 x 13 cm [⅝" x 5⅛"]
- Embroidery thread - dk brown, brown, lt brown
- Pearl cotton - beige

Instructions
1. Referring to the template/pattern and the dimensional diagram, piece, appliqué and embroider to make the front and back sections, adding specified seam allowances. Sew the front and back piece to the bottom piece to create the coin purse top. Press the seam allowances toward the bottom.
2. Cut out 1 backing and 1 batting piece the same size/shape as the top. Fuse the interfacing to the wrong side of the backing at the top opening areas (diagram 1).
3. With the top and backing right sides together, layer the batting on top of the top and sew around all edges, leaving an opening for turning right side out (diagram 2). Then, turn the piece right side out and stitch a pocket on both the front and back to hold the squeeze frame (diagram 3). Quilt as desired.
4. Fold the coin purse with right sides together, and sew the side seams (diagram 4). Top stitch the side seams close to the edge. Make the gusset (diagram 5).
5. Insert the squeeze frame inside the pockets created on the front and back pieces (diagram 6).

Dimensional Diagram

Coin purse - 1 piece each (front, bottom, back)
top fabric (appliquéd pieces) (batting)
backing (homespun)
bottom (scrap)

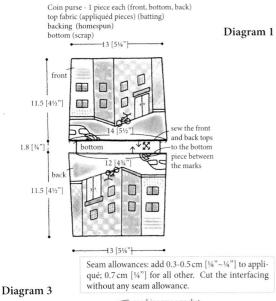

13 [5⅛"]

front

11.5 [4½"]

14 [5½"]

sew the front and back tops to the bottom piece between the marks

1.8 [¾"]

bottom

12 [4¾"]

back

11.5 [4½"]

13 [5⅛"]

Seam allowances: add 0.3-0.5 cm [⅛"~¼"] to appliqué; 0.7 cm [¼"] for all other. Cut the interfacing without any seam allowance.

Diagram 1

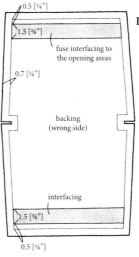

0.5 [¼"]

1.5 [⅝"]

fuse interfacing to the opening areas

0.7 [¼"]

backing (wrong side)

interfacing

1.5 [⅝"]

0.5 [¼"]

cut the backing to the same size and shape as the top, adding a 0.7 [¼"] seam allowance

Diagram 2

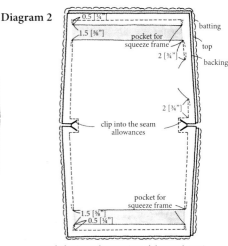

0.5 [¼"]

1.5 [⅝"]

pocket for squeeze frame

batting

top

backing

2 [¾"]

2 [¾"]

clip into the seam allowances

pocket for squeeze frame

1.5 [⅝"]

0.5 [¼"]

cut the batting to the same size and shape as the top/backing, adding a 0.7 [¼"] seam allowance; with right sides together, sew around the edges, leaving an opening

Diagram 3

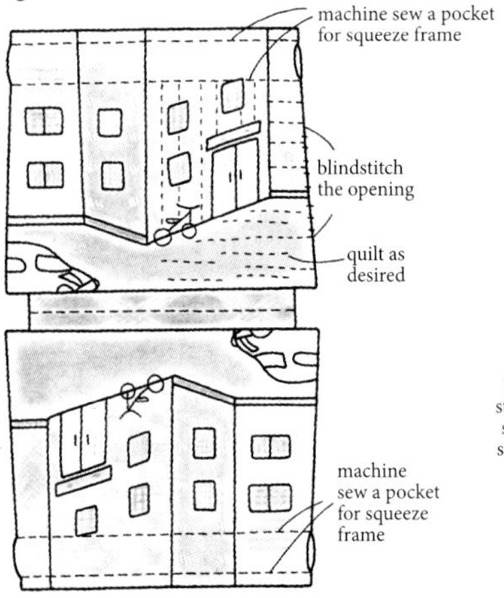

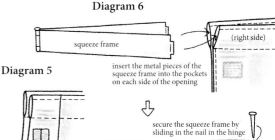

machine sew a pocket for squeeze frame

blindstitch the opening

quilt as desired

machine sew a pocket for squeeze frame

trim the batting close to stitching; turn right side out and blindstitch the opening closed; stitch 2 rows to make a pocket to hold the squeeze frame

Diagram 4

top stitch side seam

top stitch side seam

fold

fold in half with right sides out and top stitch the side seams

Diagram 5

with wrong sides together, fold the gusset flat with the side seam centered; overcast stitch together

Diagram 6

squeeze frame

(right side)

insert the metal pieces of the squeeze frame into the pockets on each side of the opening

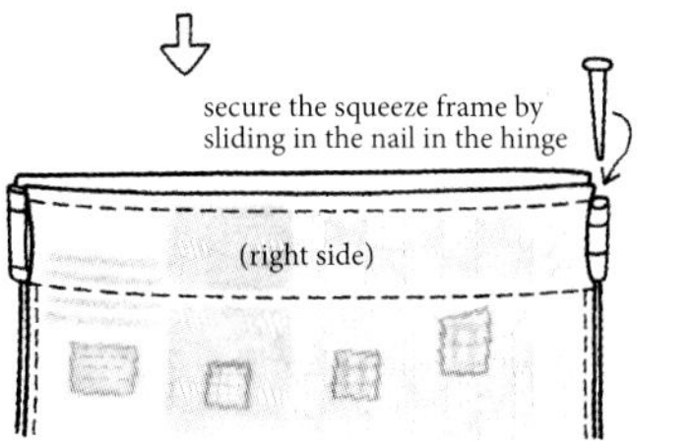

secure the squeeze frame by sliding in the nail in the hinge

(right side)

Pouch: **Loft Windows** Shown on p. 23

- The full-size template/pattern can be found on Side B of the pattern sheet inserts.
- Finished measurement: 15.5 cm [6⅛"] (w) × 10 [4"] (h); 4 cm [1½"] gusset

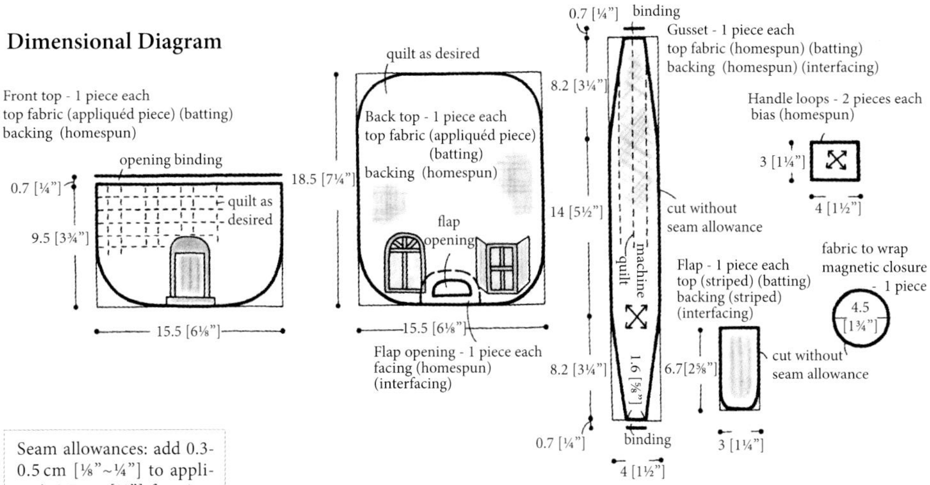

Materials Needed

Cottons

- Assorted fat quarters or scraps (appliqué)
- Striped homespun - 10 × 10 cm [4" × 4"] (flap, magnet cover)
- Homespun - 21 × 18 cm [8¼" × 7"] (back top)
- Homespun - 12 × 18 cm [4¾" × 7"] (front top)
- Homespun - 30 × 30 cm [11¾" × 11¾"] (gusset)
- Homespun - 35 × 40 cm [13¾" × 15¾"] (backing, facing)
- Homespun - 3.5 × 25 cm [1⅜" × 9¾"] (opening bias binding; 10 × 10 [4" × 4"] handle loops)
- Homespun - 3.5 × 70 cm [1⅜" × 27½"] (bias binding)
- Batting - 35 × 40 cm [13¾" × 15¾"]
- Fusible interfacing - 31 × 7 cm [12¼" × 2¾"]
- Magnetic closure - 2.5 cm [1"] diameter - 1 pair
- 2 metal D-rings - 1.2 cm [½"]
- 1 leather handle - 0.8 × 30 cm [⅜" ~ 11¾"]
- 1 spring or tongue snap - 0.8 cm [⅜"]

Dimensional Diagram

Front top - 1 piece each
top fabric (appliquéd piece) (batting)
backing (homespun)

opening binding

0.7 [¼"]

9.5 [3¾"]

quilt as desired

15.5 [6⅛"]

Back top - 1 piece each
top fabric (appliquéd piece) (batting)
backing (homespun)

quilt as desired

18.5 [7¼"]

flap opening

15.5 [6⅛"]

Flap opening - 1 piece each
facing (homespun)
(interfacing)

Gusset - 1 piece each
top fabric (homespun) (batting)
backing (homespun) (interfacing)

0.7 [¼"]   binding

8.2 [3¼"]

14 [5½"]

machine quilt

1.6 [⅝"]

8.2 [3¼"]

0.7 [¼"]   binding

4 [1½"]

Handle loops - 2 pieces each
bias (homespun)

3 [1¼"]

4 [1½"]

cut without seam allowance

Flap - 1 piece each
top (striped) (batting)
backing (striped) (interfacing)

6.7 [2⅝"]

3 [1¼"]

cut without seam allowance

fabric to wrap magnetic closure
1 piece

4.5 [1¾"]

Seam allowances: add 0.3-0.5 cm [⅛" ~ ¼"] to appliqué; 0.7 cm [¼"] for piecing; 3 cm [1¼"] for batting and backing Cut the interfacing for the flap, facing and gusset without any seam allowance, as well as the fabric for the magnetic closure and handle loops.

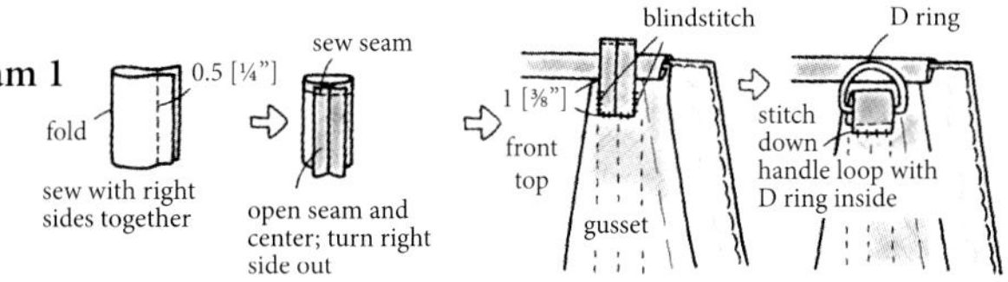

Instructions

1. Referring to the template/pattern and the dimensional diagram, piece and appliqué the front top, adding specified seam allowances. Layer the backing and top with batting in between; baste. Quilt as desired.
2. To make the gusset, fuse the interfacing to the wrong side of the backing and layer with the batting and back top; baste. Machine quilt as desired.
3. With right sides together, sew the front top and the gusset together. Trim the front and batting fabric down and use the backing to bind the raw seam allowance. Make the opening bias binding and bind the top of the front top.
4. Make the handle loops (diagram 1) and sew them to the gusset.
5. Refer to diagram 2 to make the flap and sew it above the appliqué on the front top as shown (diagram 4).
6. Appliqué the back top flap area and layer the backing and top with batting in between; baste. See diagram 3 to make the flap opening. Quilt as desired.
7. With wrong sides together, sew the front top/gusset piece to the back top, matching edges. Bind the raw edges with the bias binding. Cover the magnetic closure with fabric and sew it in position on the front top (diagram 4).

Diagram 1

fold

0.5 [¼"]

sew with right sides together

sew seam

open seam and center; turn right side out

1 [⅜"]

front top

gusset

blindstitch

D ring

stitch down handle loop with D ring inside

Diagram 2

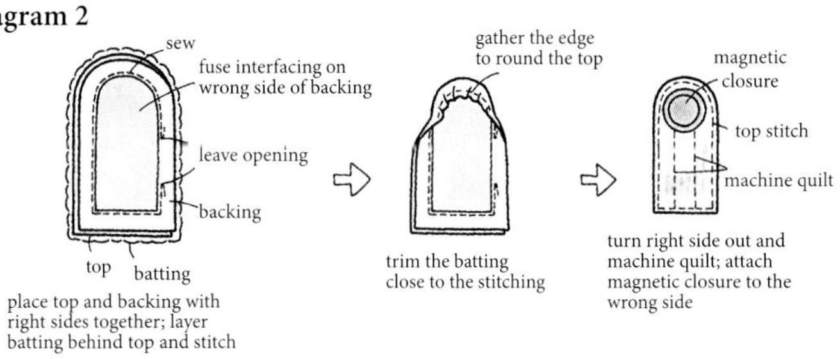

sew

fuse interfacing on wrong side of backing

leave opening

backing

top   batting

place top and backing with right sides together; layer batting behind top and stitch

gather the edge to round the top

trim the batting close to the stitching

magnetic closure

top stitch

machine quilt

turn right side out and machine quilt; attach magnetic closure to the wrong side

Diagram 3

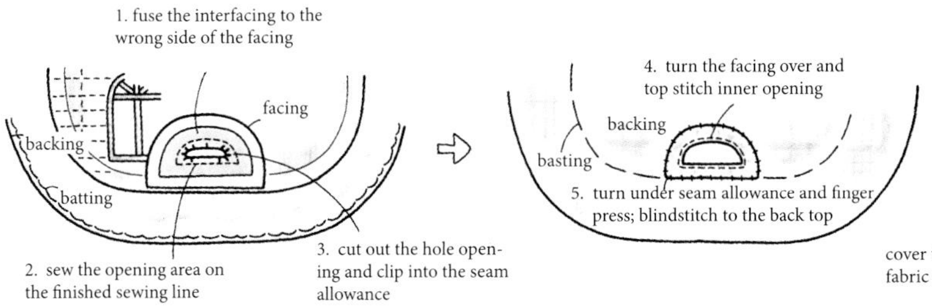

1. fuse the interfacing to the wrong side of the facing

facing

backing

batting

2. sew the opening area on the finished sewing line

3. cut out the hole opening and clip into the seam allowance

4. turn the facing over and top stitch inner opening

backing

basting

5. turn under seam allowance and finger press; blindstitch to the back top

Diagram 4

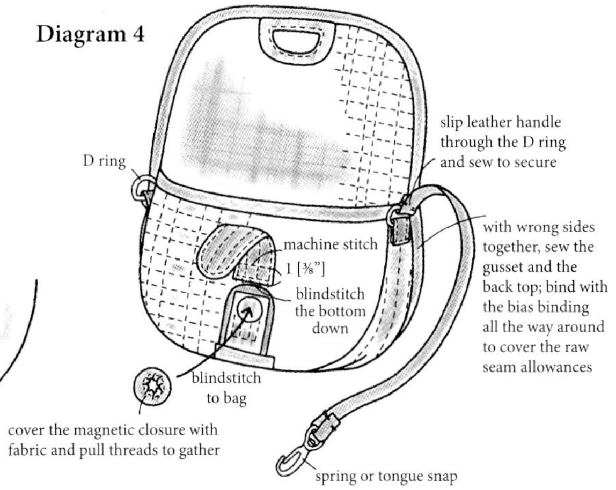

D ring

machine stitch

1 [⅜"]

blindstitch the bottom down

blindstitch to bag

cover the magnetic closure with fabric and pull threads to gather

spring or tongue snap

slip leather handle through the D ring and sew to secure

with wrong sides together, sew the gusset and the back top; bind with the bias binding all the way around to cover the raw seam allowances

Pencil Case: I'm Home! Shown on p. 23

- The full-size template/pattern can be found on Side B of the pattern sheet inserts.
- Finished measurement: 20.5 cm [8"] (w) × 9.5 cm [3¾"] (h); 6 cm [2⅜"] gusset

Materials Needed

Cottons

- Assorted fat quarters or scraps (piecing, appliqué, tabs)
- Homespun - 8 × 22 cm [3⅛"× 8⅝"] (bottom)
- Homespun - 18 × 28 cm [7"× 11"] (back top)
- Homespun - 40 × 40 cm [15¾"×15¾"] (backing, inner bias binding)
- Homespun - 3.5 × 25 cm [1⅜"× 9¾"] (bias binding)
- Homespun - 9 × 9 cm [3½"× 3½"] (tabs)
- Batting - 40 × 40 cm [15¾"×15¾"]
- 1 zipper - 17 cm [6⅝"]
- Waxed cord - 15 cm [6"] optional (zipper pull)
- Beads - optional (zipper pull)

Instructions

1. Referring to the template/pattern and the dimensional diagram, adding specified seam allowances, appliqué the front section. Then sew the front top and the back top to the bottom piece as shown in the dimensional diagram. Layer the top and backing with batting in between; baste. Quilt as desired.
2. With right sides together and center-aligned, pin the zipper tape to the front top edge and machine stitch. Turn the zipper right side out and blindstitch the edge down. Make the bias binding and bind the edge of the back top (diagram 1).
3. With right sides out, fold the piece so that the edges line up and the binding just covers the zipper; pin in place to the binding. Carefully unzip the zipper and backstitch the zipper tape to the binding on the wrong side (diagram 2).
4. Make the tabs (diagram 3) and baste them to both ends of the zipper (diagram 2). They will be sewn into the side seams.
5. Turn the case inside out and sew the sides. Trim the top and batting down to 0.7 cm [¼"]. Use the backing fabric to bind the raw seam allowances on either side.
6. Make a 2.5 cm [1"] bias binding. Sew the upper and lower gusset corners; trim and bind the seam allowances with the binding (see p. 69 for detailed instructions).
7. Turn right side out. Make a zipper pull from the waxed cord and beads; slip through and tie off on the zipper clasp.

Dimensional Diagram

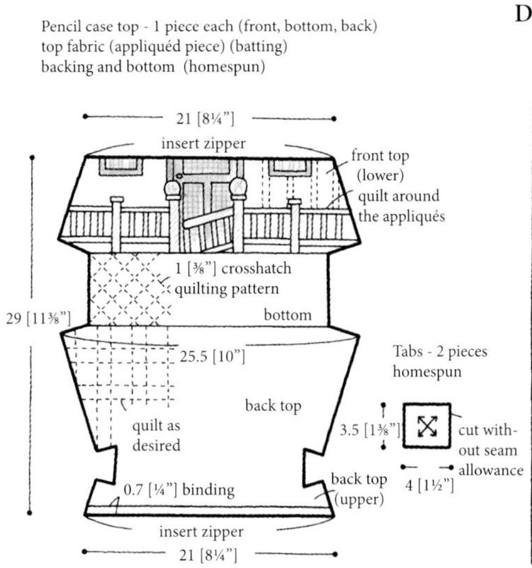

Pencil case top - 1 piece each (front, bottom, back)
top fabric (appliquéd piece) (batting)
backing and bottom (homespun)

21 [8¼"]
insert zipper
front top (lower)
quilt around the appliqués
1 [⅜"] crosshatch quilting pattern
bottom
29 [11⅜"]
25.5 [10"]
back top
quilt as desired
3.5 [1⅜"]
back top (upper)
4 [1½"]
0.7 [¼"] binding
insert zipper
21 [8¼"]

Tabs - 2 pieces homespun
cut without seam allowance

Seam allowances: add 0.3-0.5 cm [⅛"~¼"] to appliqué; 0.7 cm [¼"] for pieces; 3 cm [1¼"] for batting and backing. Cut the tabs without any seam allowance.

Diagram 1

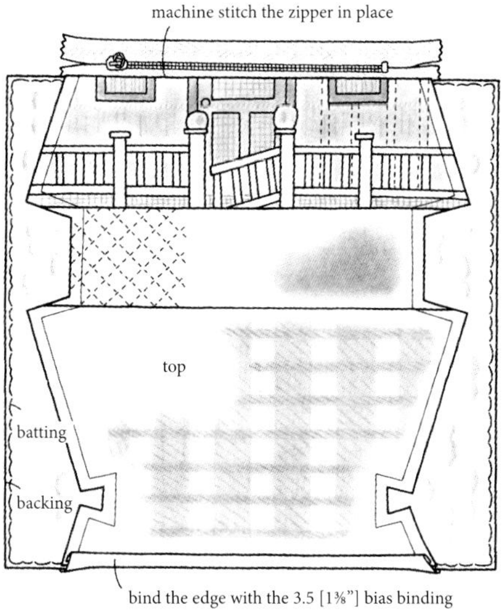

machine stitch the zipper in place
top
batting
backing
bind the edge with the 3.5 [1⅜"] bias binding

Diagram 2

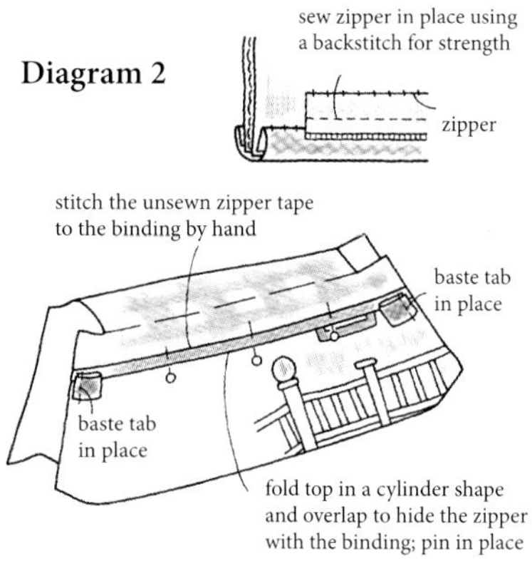

sew zipper in place using a backstitch for strength
zipper
stitch the unsewn zipper tape to the binding by hand
baste tab in place
baste tab in place
fold top in a cylinder shape and overlap to hide the zipper with the binding; pin in place

Diagram 3

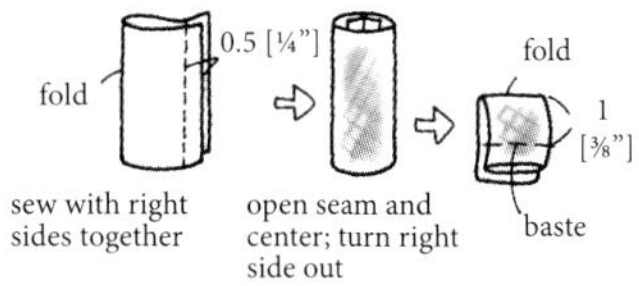

fold
0.5 [¼"]
fold
1 [⅜"]
sew with right sides together
open seam and center; turn right side out
baste

Diagram 4

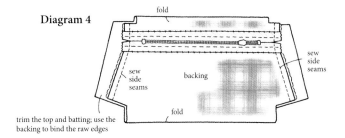

fold
sew side seams
sew side seams
backing
fold
trim the top and batting; use the backing to bind the raw edges

Diagram 5

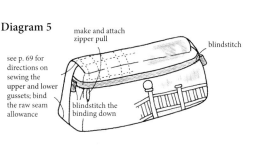

make and attach zipper pull
blindstitch
see p. 69 for directions on sewing the upper and lower gussets; bind the raw seam allowance
blindstitch the binding down

Pouch: **In the Woods**   Shown on p. 24

- The full-size template/pattern can be found on Side B of the pattern sheet inserts.
- Finished measurement: 12.5 cm [4⅞"] (diameter); 3 cm [1¼"] gusset

Materials Needed
Cottons
- Assorted fat quarters or scraps (piecing, appliqué, tabs)
- Beige print - 25 × 55 cm [9⅞" × 21⅝"] (top, gusset A, B)
- Homespun - 35 × 55 cm [13¾" × 21⅝"] (backing, bias binding)
- Homespun - 8 × 8 cm [3⅛" × 3⅛"] (tabs)
- Batting - 20 × 70 cm [7⅞" × 27½"]
- Fusible interfacing - 3 × 24 cm [1¼" × 9⅜"]
- Leather or suede handles - 1 × 28 cm [⅜" × 11"] 2 pieces
- 1 zipper - 13 cm [5⅛"]
- Leather cord - 15 cm [6"] optional (zipper pull) green
- Beads - optional (zipper pull)
- Embroidery thread - black, orange

Instructions
1. Referring to the template/pattern and the dimensional diagram, piece the left, center and right sections for both the front and back of the pouch, adding specified seam allowances. For each of the individual sections, layer the top and backing with batting in between; baste. Quilt as desired.
2. With right sides together, sew the left side, center and right sections together (diagram 1) to create 2 half-circle sections. Cut the handle leather into 2 equal pieces. Baste the handles to the right sides of the front and back sections (diagram 2).
3. Refer to diagram 3 to make gusset A and diagram 4 to make gusset B.
4. Make a 2.5 cm [1"] bias binding out of the backing fabric and sew to each side of the zipper tape (see p. 62, 63 for detailed directions). Make the tabs (diagram 5) and baste them on both ends of gusset A. Sew gussets A and B together to form a cylinder shape.
5. With right sides together, sew the front section to the gusset, centering the zipper and the handles; repeat to sew the back section of the bag to the gusset. Use the bias binding to bind the raw seam allowances. Turn pouch inside out. Make a zipper pull from the leather cord and beads; slip through and tie off on the zipper clasp.

Dimensional Diagram

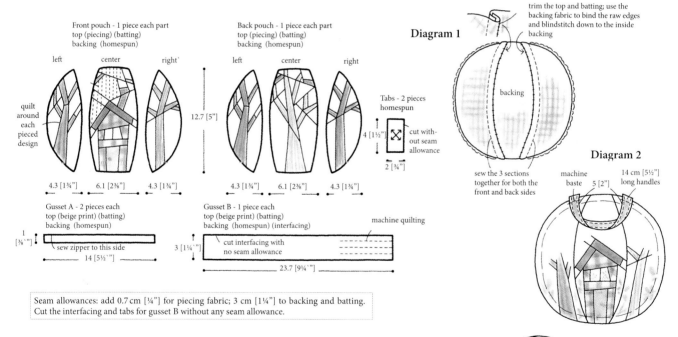

Seam allowances: add 0.7 cm [¼"] for piecing fabric; 3 cm [1¼"] to backing and batting.
Cut the interfacing and tabs for gusset B without any seam allowance.

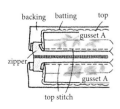

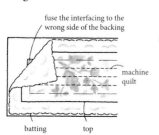

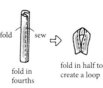

Pouch: Flying High in the Sky

Shown on p. 25

- The full-size pattern can be found below.
- Finished measurement:
  19 cm [7½"] (w) × 11.5 cm [4½"] (h); 3.5 cm [1⅜"] gusset

Materials Needed

Cottons
- Assorted fat quarters or scraps (appliqué)
- Print - 15 ×50 cm [5⅞"× 19⅝"] (top)
- Homespun- 5 ×30 cm [2"×11¾"] (gusset top)
- Homespun- 40×60 cm [15¾"× 23⅝"] (backing, inner bias binding)
- Print-3.5×50 cm [1⅜"× 19⅝"] (bias binding)
- Batting - 30 ×60 cm [11¾"× 23⅝"]
- Fusible interfacing - 4 ×28 cm [1½"× 11"]
- 1 zipper - 18 cm [7"]
- Waxed cord - 15 cm [6"] optional (zipper pull)
- Beads - optional (zipper pull)
- Embroidery thread - black, dk beige, grey

Instructions

1. Referring to the pattern and the dimensional diagram below, piece, appliqué and embroider to make the front and back sections, adding specified seam allowances. Layer the top and backing with batting in between; baste. Quilt as desired. Refer to the pattern to make the pleats; baste.
2. Fuse the interfacing to the wrong side of the gusset backing and layer with the gusset top and batting. Machine quilt.
3. With right sides together, sew the bag front and back to the gusset, matching edges. Make a 2.5 cm [1"] wide bias binding from the same fabric as the backing and bind the raw seam allowances on the inside of the pouch.
4. Make a 3.5 cm [1⅜"] wide bias binding to bind the opening. Sew the zipper to the opening (backstitch the tapes to the underside of the opening binding). Attach zipper pull.

Seam allowances: add 0.3-0.5 cm [⅛"~¼"] to appliqué; 0.7 cm [¼"] for pieces; 3 cm [1¼"] for batting and backing. Cut the gusset interfacing without any seam allowance.

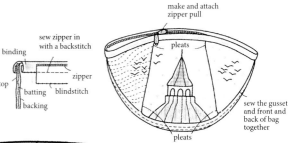

Dimensional Diagram

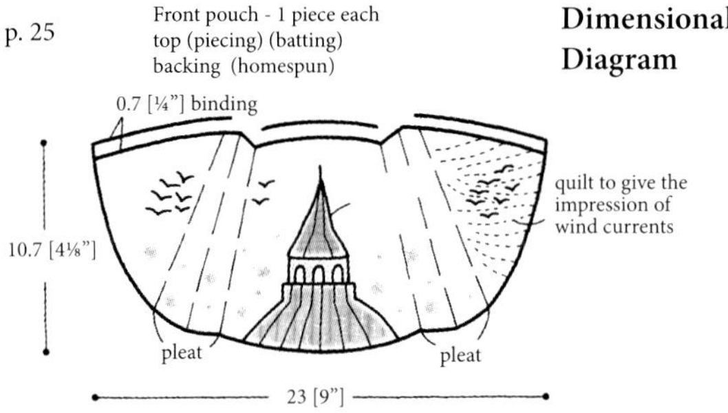

Front pouch - 1 piece each
top (piecing) (batting)
backing (homespun)

0.7 [¼"] binding

quilt to give the impression of wind currents

10.7 [4⅛"]

pleat   pleat

23 [9"]

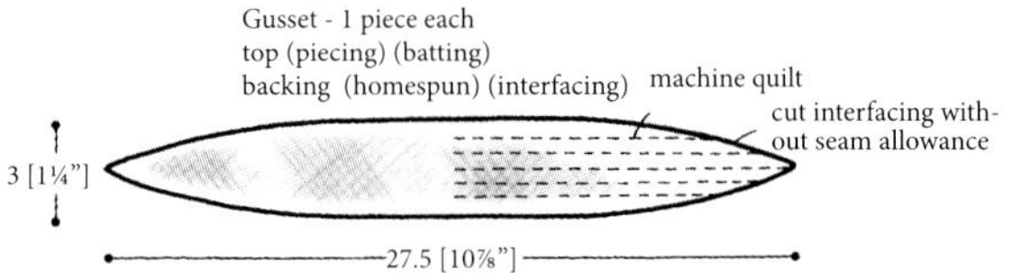

Gusset - 1 piece each
top (piecing) (batting)
backing (homespun) (interfacing)   machine quilt

cut interfacing without seam allowance

3 [1¼"]

27.5 [10⅞"]

make and attach zipper pull

sew zipper in with a backstitch

binding

top

zipper

blindstitch

batting

backing

pleats

pleats

sew the gusset and front and back of bag together

Full-size Pattern and Design

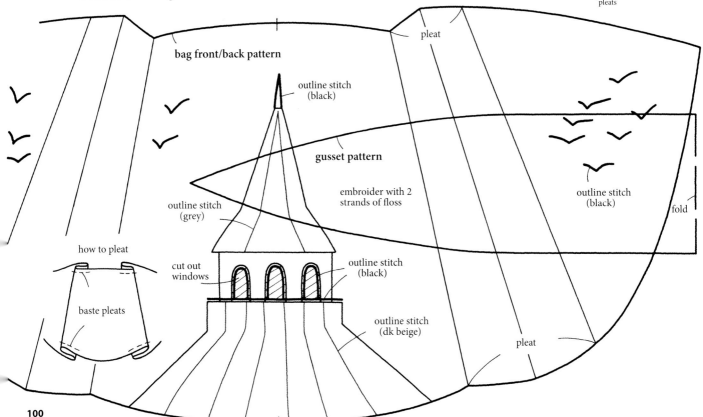

bag front/back pattern

outline stitch (black)

gusset pattern

embroider with 2 strands of floss

outline stitch (grey)

outline stitch (black)

fold

how to pleat

cut out windows

outline stitch (black)

baste pleats

outline stitch (dk beige)

pleat

pleat

Placemats: **Snow Falling • An Autumn Breeze**   Shown on p. 28

• The pattern for "Snow Falling" can be found below • The pattern for "Autumn Breeze" can be found on Side C of the pattern sheet inserts.
• Finished measurement: 39.4 cm [15½"] (w) × 29.4 cm [11⅜"] (h)

Materials Needed (for one placemat)
Cottons
- Assorted fat quarters or scraps (appliqué)
- Print - 30 × 40 cm [11¾" × 15¾"] (top)
- Print - 32 × 42 cm [12⅝"× 16½"] (backing)
- Print- 3.5 × 135 cm [1⅜"× 53¼"] (bias binding)
- Batting - 32 × 42 cm [12⅝"× 16½"]]
- Embroidery thread - olive, gray, lt beige

Instructions
1. Referring to the pattern and the dimensional diagram below, cut out the background and appliqués, adding specified seam allowances. The appliqués should be stitched down in the following order: house pieces "a" and "b", cross "c", belfry "d", house "e", windows and door. Next, appliqué the trees, the ground and add embroidery. All techniques are explained in detail on p. 51-58.
2. Layer the top and backing with batting in between; baste. Quilt as desired.
3. Bind the edges to finish the placemat.

> Seam allowances: add 0.3-0.5 cm [⅛"~¼"] to appliqué; 0.7 cm [¼"] for pieces; 2 cm [¾"] for batting and backing.

Dimensional Diagram "Snow Falling"

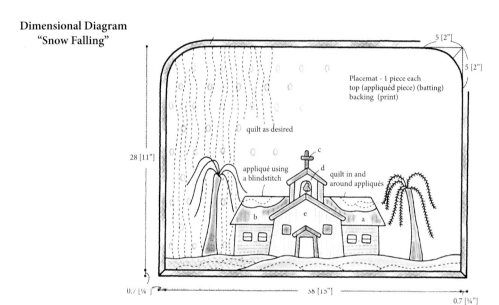

5 [2"]

5 [2"]

Placemat - 1 piece each
top (appliquéd piece) (batting)
backing (print)

quilt as desired

appliqué using a blindstitch

quilt in and around appliqués

28 [11"]

0.7 [¼"]   38 [15"]   0.7 [¼"]

The dimensions and basic construction for the project "An Autumn Breeze" is the same as that of "Snow Falling." The appliqué design can be found on Side C of the pattern sheet inserts.

Pattern and Design

Appliqué design
*Pattern below is 50% of actual size. Enlarge the design 200% using a copy machine to obtain the full-size template.

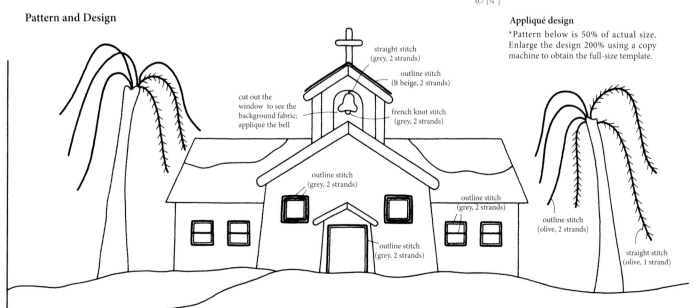

straight stitch (grey, 2 strands)

outline stitch (lt beige, 2 strands)

cut out the window to see the background fabric; appliqué the bell

french knot stitch (grey, 2 strands)

outline stitch (grey, 2 strands)

outline stitch (grey, 2 strands)

outline stitch (grey, 2 strands)

outline stitch (olive, 2 strands)

outline stitch (grey, 2 strands)

straight stitch (olive, 1 strand)

101

Tea Cozy: A Holiday Cottage Shown on p. 29

- The full-size template/pattern can be found on Side D of the pattern sheet inserts.
- Finished measurement: 22 cm [8⅝"] (w) × 18 cm [7"] (h); 14 cm [5½"] (d)

Materials Needed
Cottons
- 30 assorted fat quarters or scraps (piecing, appliqué)
- Homespun - 50 ×55 cm [19⅝"×21⅝"] (backing - not including chimney)
- Print- 7×18 cm [2¾"×7"] (chimney top)
- Homespun - 20 ×10 cm [7⅞"×4"] (backing for chimney)
- Homespun - 3.5×75 cm [1⅜"×29½"] (bias binding for house)
- Homespun - 3.5×85 cm [1⅜"×33½"] (bias binding for roof)
- Homespun - 3.5×20 cm [1⅜"×7⅞"] (bias binding for chimney)
- Batting - 50 ×55 cm [19⅝"×21⅝"]
- Embroidery thread - dk brown, dk grey

Instructions
1. Referring to the full-size template/pattern and the dimensional diagram, cut out pattern pieces and appliqués, adding specified seam allowances.
2. Piece each of the 4 sides (front, back, left and right) and add appliqués and embroidery.
3. For each of the 4 pieces, lay the top and backing with right sides together and lay them on top of the batting, matching edges. Sew around 3 sides, leaving the bottom open. Trim batting close to stitching; turn right side out and press. Quilt as desired (diagram 1).
4. With right sides out, overcast stitch the 4 sides of the house together. Bind the bottom raw edges of the house.
5. Piece the roof top together as shown in the dimensional diagram. Layer the top and backing with batting in between; baste. Quilt as desired. Bind the bottom raw edges of the roof.
6. Make the chimney (diagram 2). Blindstitch the chimney to the roof.
7. Blindstitch the roof to the house.

Seam allowances: add 0.3-0.5 cm [⅛"~¼"] to appliqué; 0.7 cm [¼"] for all other fabric

Dimensional Diagram

Chimney - 1 piece each
top (print) (batting)
backing (homespun)

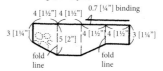

4 [1½"] 4 [1½"]   0.7 [¼"] binding
3 [1¼"] 4 [1½"] 4 [1½"] 3 [1¼"]
5 [2"]
fold line   fold line

Roof - 1 piece each
top (piecing) (batting)
backing (homespun)

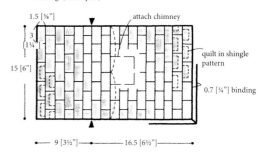

1.5 [⅝"]   attach chimney
3 [1¼"]
15 [6"]   quilt in shingle pattern
0.7 [¼"] binding
9 [3½"]   16.5 [6½"]

Front - 1 piece each
top (appliquéd piecing) (batting)
backing (homespun)

Right side - 1 piece each
top (appliquéd piecing) (batting)
backing (homespun)

13.5 [5⅜"]   10 [4"]
0.7 [¼"] binding
22 [8⅝"]   14 [5½"]

Back - 1 piece each
top (appliquéd piecing) (batting)
backing (homespun)

Left side - 1 piece each
top (appliquéd piecing) (batting)
backing (homespun)

10 [4"]   13.5 [5⅜"]
0.7 [¼"] binding
22 [8⅝"]   14 [5½"]

Diagram 1 - Making the Sides

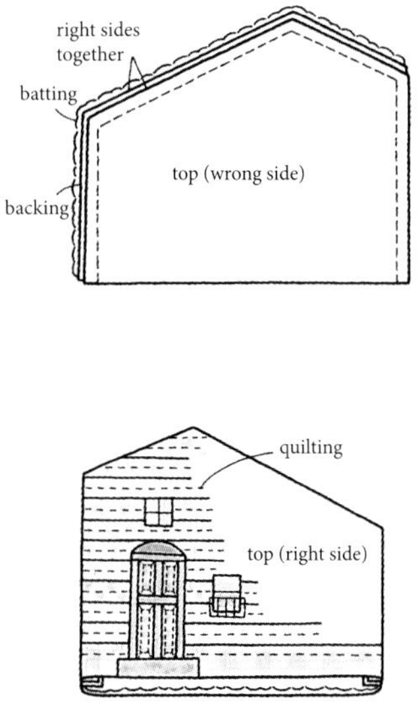

right sides together
batting
top (wrong side)
backing

finished tea cozy

blindstitch the chimney to the roof

quilting
top (right side)

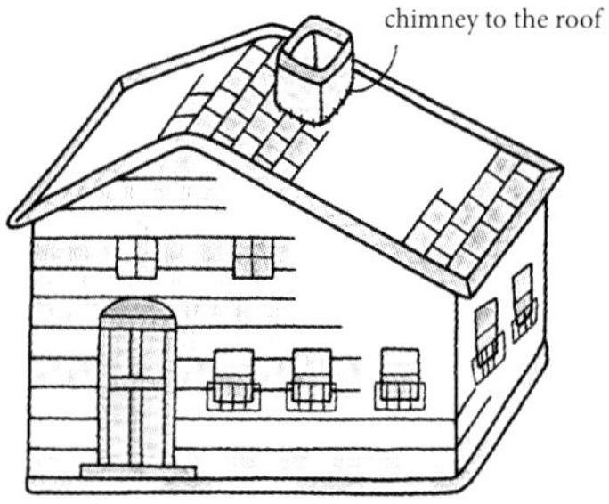

Diagram 2 - Making the Chimney

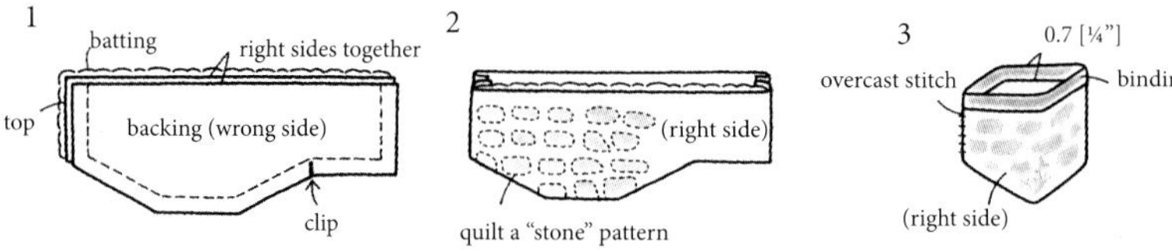

1
batting   right sides together
top
backing (wrong side)
clip

2
(right side)
quilt a "stone" pattern

3
0.7 [¼"]
overcast stitch   binding
(right side)

Pillows: Houses in a Foreign Country Shown on p. 30, 31

- The pattern can be found below.
- Finished measurement:
  (Pillow A) 23.5 × 24 cm [9¼" × 9⅜"]
  (Pillow B) 22 × 37 cm [8⅝" × 14½"]

Dimensional Diagram

Pillow A top (pieced wool) - 1 piece
4 [1½"] pom poms
stitch to the top of triangle
appliqué to top using a buttonhole stitch (4 strands)
23.5 [9¼"]
5 [2"] leave open 5 [2"]
24 [9½"]

backing (wool) 1 piece
24 [9½"]

Pillow B top (pieced wool) - 1 piece
buttonhole stitch 5 [2"] pom pom
23.5 [9¼"]
37 [14½"]

backing (wool) 1 piece
on fold
24 [9⅜"]

Materials Needed (Pillow A)
Wool
- Assorted scraps (piecing, appliqué)
- Wool - 25 × 26 cm [9¾" × 10¼"] backing)
- 3 Pom Poms - 4 cm [1½"] in diameter
- Embroidery thread - green, moss green, grey, beige, dk brown
- Pillow form - 26 cm [10¼"]

* to fit U.S. size pillow forms, enlarge the pattern slightly and use a 12" sq. form, or make your own using polyester filling

Materials Needed (Pillow B)
Wool
- Assorted scraps (piecing, appliqué)
- Wool - 25 × 40 cm [9¾" × 15¾"] backing)
- 1 Pom Pom - 5 cm [2"] in diameter
- Embroidery thread - black, dk brown
- Pearl cotton - mustard, blue, wine red
- Pillow form - 24 × 39 cm [9½" × 15⅜"]

* to fit U.S. size pillow forms, enlarge the pattern slightly larger and use a 9" x 16" form, or make your own using polyester filling

Seam allowances: add 0.3-0.5 cm [⅛"~¼"] to appliqué; 0.7 cm [¼"] for all other fabric

Instructions
(Pillow A)

1. Referring to the full-size template/pattern and the dimensional diagram, cut out pattern pieces and appliqués, adding specified seam allowances.
2. Sew the rectangles together, side by side. Then sew the 7 triangles together as shown in the dimensional diagram. Sew the triangle to the top of the rectangles to create the top of the pillow.
3. Appliqué the windows and doors to the top using a blanket stitch.
4. With right sides together, sew the top and backing together leaving an opening to insert the pillow form. Turn right side out; insert the pillow form and blindstitch the opening closed.
5. Sew the pom poms to the tops of the triangles.

* Follow the steps above to make Pillow B.

Appliqué design

*Pattern below is 50% of actual size. Enlarge the design 200% using a copy machine to obtain the full-size template.

Pattern and Design

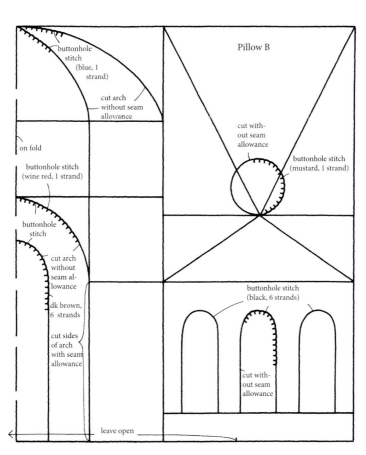

buttonhole stitch (blue, 1 strand)
cut arch without seam allowance
on fold
buttonhole stitch (wine red, 1 strand)
buttonhole stitch
cut arch without seam allowance
dk brown, 6 strands
cut sides of arch with seam allowance
leave open

Pillow B
cut without seam allowance
buttonhole stitch (mustard, 1 strand)
buttonhole stitch (black, 6 strands)
cut without seam allowance

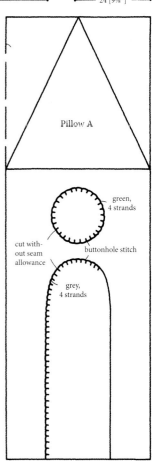

Pillow A
green, 4 strands
cut without seam allowance
buttonhole stitch
grey, 4 strands

103

Tray: **My Hometown** Shown on p. 32

- The full-size template/pattern can be found on Side C of the pattern sheet inserts.
- Finished measurement: 15 × 22 cm [5⅞" × 8⅝"]

Materials Needed

Cottons

- Assorted fat quarters or scraps (piecing, appliqué)
- Homespun - 25 ×60 cm [9⅞"×23⅝"] backing)
- Muslin- 25 ×60 cm [9⅞"×23⅝"] (facing)
- Print - 30 ×25 cm [11¾"×9⅞"] (streets, bottom top fabric)
- Batting - 40 ×50 cm [15¾"× 19¾"]
- Fusible interfacing - 30 ×22 cm [11¾"×8⅝"]
- Clear plastic template - 23 ×37 cm [9"×14½"]
- 1 toothpick - for the core of the cross

Instructions

1. Referring to the full-size template/pattern and the dimensional diagram, cut out pattern pieces and appliqués, adding specified seam allowances.
2. Piece and appliqué each of the 4 sides (A-D). For each of the 4 pieces, layer the top and facing with batting in between; baste. Quilt as desired. Mark the finished sewing lines on the wrong side.
3. Then, lay the quilted piece and backing with right sides together, matching edges. Sew around 3 sides, leaving the bottom open. Trim batting close to stitching; turn right side out and press (diagram 1). Cut the clear template plastic to fit each side. Insert the matching plastic piece into the quilted side from the open bottom (diagram 2).
4. To make the bottom, fuse the interfacing to the wrong side of the facing. Layer the bottom top and the facing with batting in between; baste. Quilt as shown or as desired. With right sides together, sew the bottom to the 4 sides (diagram 3).
5. Make the inner bottom (diagram 4). Place it on the inside bottom and blindstitch in place, sewing along the seams made in step 4.
6. Lift up the sides and sew them together with an overcast stitch (diagram 5). Make the chimneys (diagram 6) and the cross (diagram 7) and blindstitch them to the rooftops.

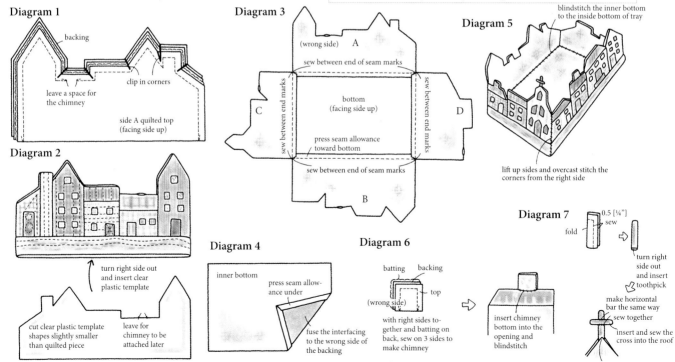

Sides A~D - 1 piece each side
top (piecing) (batting)
facing (muslin)
backing (homespun)
clear template plastic

Dimensional Diagram

A

Cross - 2 pieces (print)
cut without seam allowance

10 [4"]
3 [1¼"]
2 [¾"]
1.5 [⅝"]

D

cut interfacing without seam allowance
1 [⅜"] crosshatch quilting pattern

quilt as desired
quilt in and around houses

C

Bottom - 1 piece each
top (print) (batting)
facing (muslin) (interfacing)
backing (homespun) (interfacing)

15 [5⅞"]

8.5 [3⅜"]   1.5 [⅝"]   1.5 [⅝"]   22 [8⅝"]   1.5 [⅝"]   11 [4⅜"]

10 [4"]

B

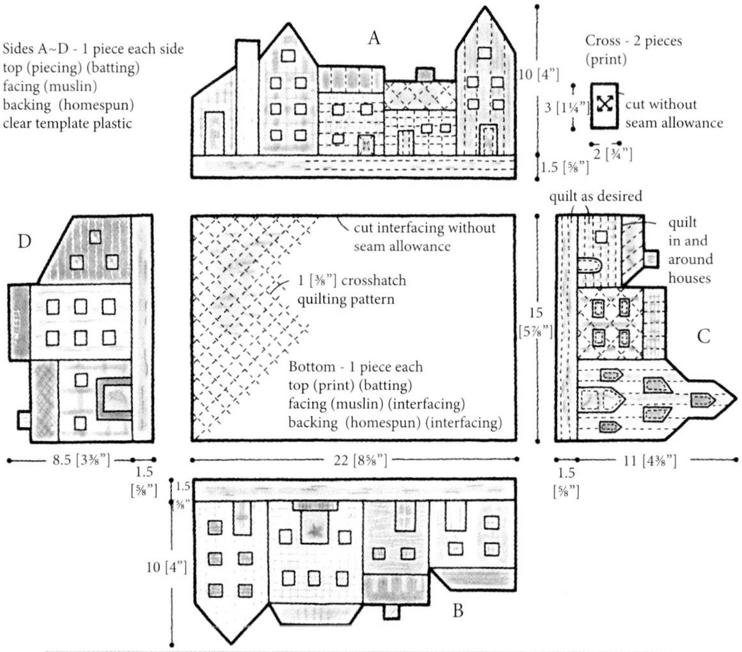

Seam allowances: add 0.3-0.5 cm [⅛"~¼"] to appliqué; 0.7 cm [¼"] for all other fabric; cut the interfacing and clear plastic template without seam allowance

Diagram 1

backing
clip in corners
leave a space for the chimney
side A quilted top (facing side up)

Diagram 2

turn right side out and insert clear plastic template
cut clear plastic template shapes slightly smaller than quilted piece
leave for chimney to be attached later

Diagram 3

(wrong side) A
sew between end of seam marks
C
sew between end of seam marks
bottom (facing side up)
D
sew between end of seam marks
press seam allowance toward bottom
sew between end of seam marks
B

Diagram 4

inner bottom
press seam allowance under
fuse the interfacing to the wrong side of the backing

Diagram 5

blindstitch the inner bottom to the inside bottom of tray
lift up sides and overcast stitch the corners from the right side

Diagram 6

batting   backing
top
(wrong side)
with right sides together and batting on back, sew on 3 sides to make chimney
insert chimney bottom into the opening and blindstitch

Diagram 7

0.5 [¼"] sew
fold
turn right side out and insert toothpick
make horizontal bar the same way
sew together
insert and sew the cross into the roof

Magazine Holder: **A Town on a Hill** Shown on p. 33

- The template/pattern can be found on Side D of the pattern sheet inserts.
- Finished measurement:
  40 cm [15¾"] (w)
  26 cm [10¼"] (h)
  27 cm [10⅝"] (d)

Dimensional Diagram

Materials Needed

Cottons

- Assorted fat quarters or scraps (piecing, appliqué)
- Homespun - 50 ×75 cm [19¾" ×29½"] (top)
- Striped homespun- 10 ×75 cm [4"×29½"] (opening)
- Homespun - 81 ×94 cm [31⅞"×37"] (backing)
- Homespun - 8 ×30 cm [3⅛"×11¾"] (handle loops)
- Muslin - 81 ×94 cm [31⅞"×37"] (facing)
- Corduroy - 45 ×45 cm [17¾"×17¾"] (bottom, street)
- Batting - 110 × 160 cm [43¼"× 1¾ yds]
- Fusible interfacing - 6 × 10 cm [2⅜"× 4"]
- Binder board - 70 ×80 cm [27½"×31½"]
- Wooden handle - 1 pair

Instructions

1. Refer to the template/pattern and the dimensional diagram, cut out pattern pieces and appliqués, adding specified seam allowances.
2. Piece and appliqué each of the 4 sides (A-D), working from the building in the back, forward. Sew the sides and bottom together to make 1 large quilt top. Layer the top and facing with batting in between; baste. Quilt as desired.
3. Then, lay the quilted piece and backing with right sides together, matching edges. Sew the "v" of each side, leaving the bottoms open (diagram 1).
4. Trim batting close to stitching; turn right side out. Top stitch the perimeter of the bottom on 3 sides (diagram 2). Measure the bottom and all 4 sides; cut each piece of board 0.3 [⅛"] smaller. Wrap each board with batting and whipstitch (diagram 3).
5. Insert the board into the bottom first; either stitch by hand or use a zipper foot to stitch close to the board to secure the seam. Then insert the boards for the sides.
6. Make the handle loops (diagram 4) and put them through the handles, folding them in half and basting.
7. Turn the seam allowances under on the opening sides of C and D; sandwich the handle loops in position and securely stitch in place. Blindstitch the openings for all 4 sides.
8. Lift up the sides and sew the edges together from the right side using a overcast stitch (diagram 5).

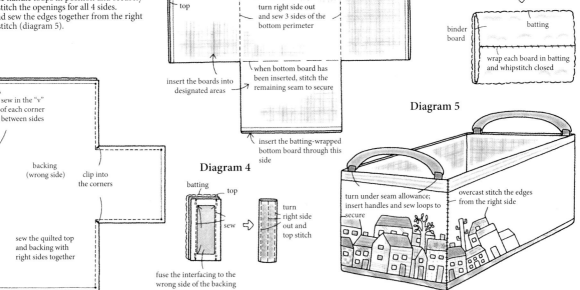

Sides A~D - 1 piece each side
top (piecing) (batting)
facing (muslin)
backing (homespun)
clear template plastic

26 [10¼"]

A

Handle loops - 4 pieces each
top (homespun)
backing (homespun) (interfacing)

6 [2⅜"] cut without
seam allowance

2.2 [⅞"]

D

27
[10⅝"]

20 [7⅞"]

handle position

2

Bottom - 1 piece each
(corduroy)

3 [1¼"] crosshatch
quilting pattern

40 [15¾"]

27
[10⅝"]

20 [7⅞"]

handle position

C

quilt in and around
buildings; quilt other
areas as desired

26 [10¼"]

B

Seam allowances: add
0.3-0.5 cm [⅛"~¼"] to
appliqué; 0.7 cm [¼"]
for all other fabric; cut
the handle loops without seam allowance.

26 [10¼"]   40 [15¾"]   26 [10¼"]

Diagram 2

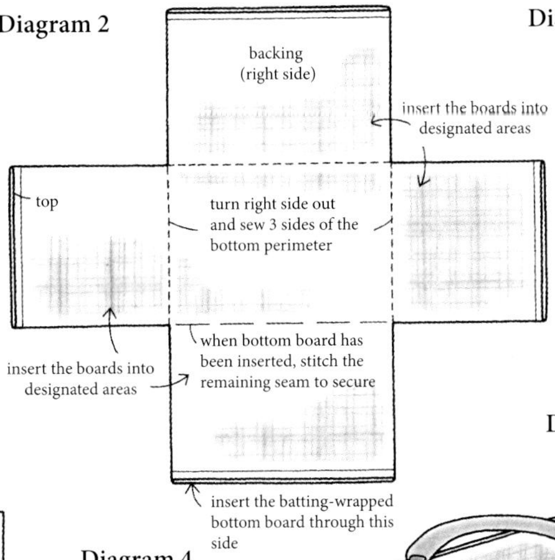

backing
(right side)

insert the boards into
designated areas

top

turn right side out
and sew 3 sides of the
bottom perimeter

insert the boards into
designated areas

when bottom board has
been inserted, stitch the
remaining seam to secure

insert the batting-wrapped
bottom board through this
side

Diagram 3

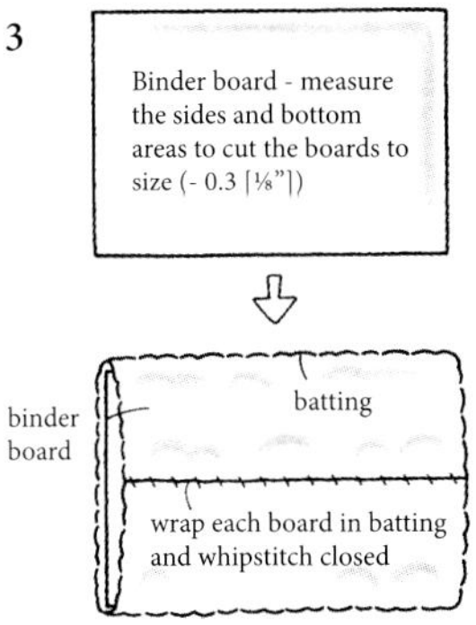

Binder board - measure
the sides and bottom
areas to cut the boards to
size (- 0.3 [⅛"])

binder
board

batting

wrap each board in batting
and whipstitch closed

Diagram 1

sew in the "v"
of each corner
between sides

sew in the "v"
of each corner
between sides

top

backing
(wrong side)

clip into
the corners

0.7 [¼"]

sew the quilted top
and backing with
right sides together

Diagram 4

batting   top

fuse the interfacing to the
wrong side of the backing

turn
right side
out and
top stitch

sew

Diagram 5

turn under seam allowance;
insert handles and sew loops to
secure

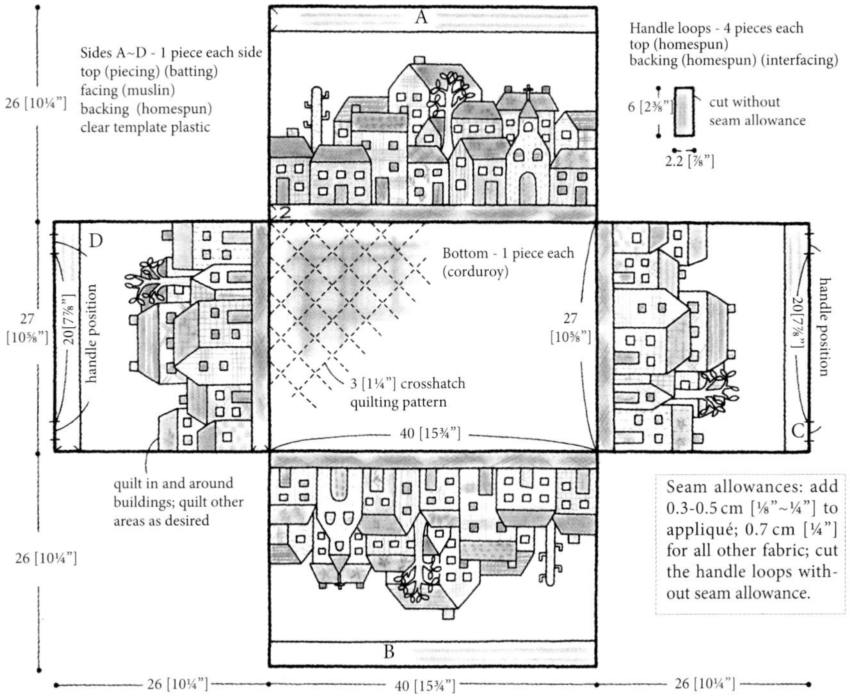

overcast stitch the edges
from the right side

Soft Blocks: **House-Shaped Blocks** Shown on p. 34

- The full-size template/pattern can be found on Side C of the pattern sheet inserts.
- Finished measurement: see individual finished diagrams

Materials Needed (House A)

Cottons
- Assorted fat quarters or scraps (appliqué)
- Striped homespun A - 15 × 42 cm [5⅞" × 16½"] (house top)
- Striped homespun B - 19 × 18 cm [7½" × 7"] (roof top, backing)
- Homespun - 8 × 13 cm [3⅛" × 5⅛"] (bottom)
- Print - 11 × 10 cm [4⅜" × 4"] (chimney)
- Muslin - 15 × 42 cm [5⅞" × 16½"] (backing)
- Batting - 15 × 75 cm [5⅞" × 29½"]
- Fusible interfacing - 7 × 17 cm [2¾" × 6⅝"] (medium)
                        6 × 12 cm [2⅜" × 4¾"] (heavyweight)
- Polyester filling - to fill house
- Embroidery thread - yellow, dk brown

Instructions

1. Refer to each step from 1 ~ 11 to make House A. Follow the same directions to make the similar House B and House C.

Seam allowances: add 0.3-0.5 cm [⅛"~¼"] to appliqué; 0.7 cm [¼"] for all other pieces; cut the interfacing without any seam allowances.

Dimensional Diagram
House A

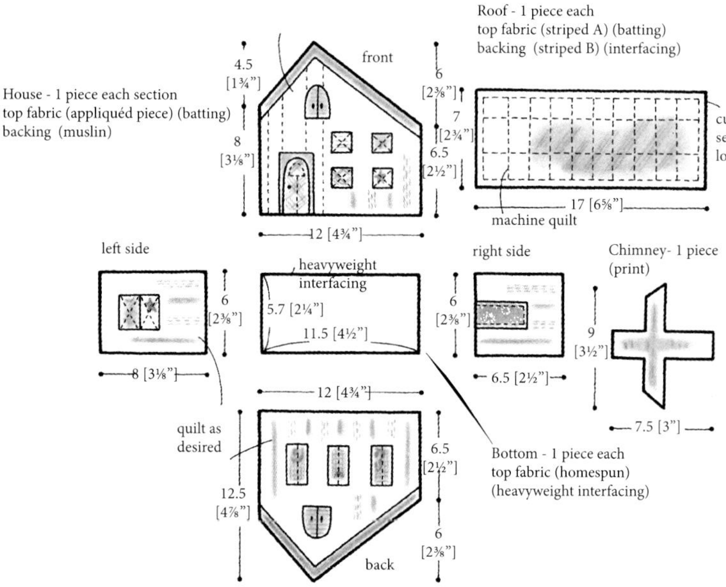

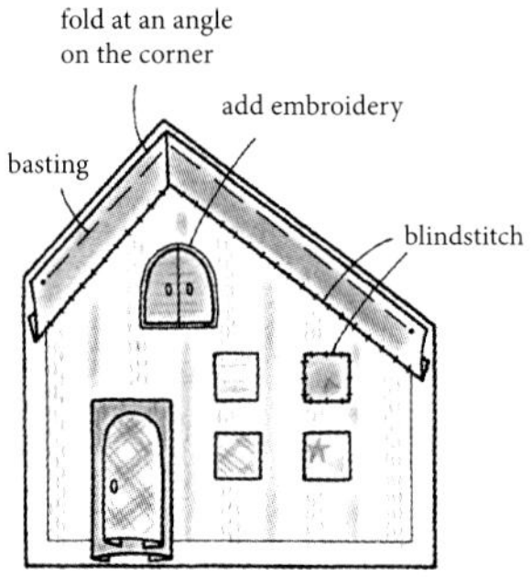

House - 1 piece each section
top fabric (appliquéd piece) (batting)
backing (muslin)

Roof - 1 piece each
top fabric (striped A) (batting)
backing (striped B) (interfacing)

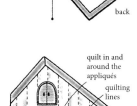

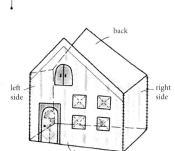

front

4.5 [1¾"]

8 [3⅛"]

12 [4¾"]

6 [2⅜"]
7 [2¾"]
6.5 [2½"]

cut without seam allowance

17 [6⅝"]
machine quilt

left side

6 [2⅜"]

8 [3⅛"]

right side

6 [2⅜"]

6.5 [2½"]

Chimney - 1 piece (print)

9 [3½"]

7.5 [3"]

heavyweight interfacing

5.7 [2¼"]

11.5 [4½"]

12 [4¾"]

quilt as desired

12.5 [4⅞"]

6.5 [2½"]

6 [2⅜"]

back

Bottom - 1 piece each
top fabric (homespun)
(heavyweight interfacing)

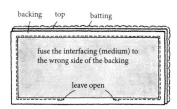

fold at an angle on the corner

add embroidery

basting

blindstitch

1. Add appliqués and embroidery to the top fabric for all 4 sides of the house.

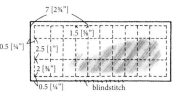

top (wrong side)

backing

batting

leave open

2. Place the quilt top and backing right sides together and layer on top of the batting. Sew around the edges, leaving the bottom open.

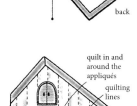

quilt in and around the appliqués

quilting lines

3. Trim the batting close to the stitching and turn right side out. Quilt as desired. Repeat for all 4 sides.

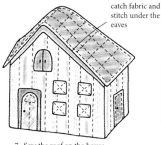

back

left side

right side

front

4. With right sides out, sew each of the 4 sides together with a overcast stitch; catch only the top fabric as you sew.

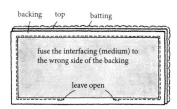

backing   top   batting

fuse the interfacing (medium) to the wrong side of the backing

leave open

5. To make the roof, place the top and backing right sides together and layer on top of the batting; sew around the edges, leaving an opening.

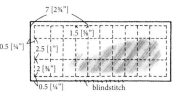

0.5 [¼"]

7 [2¾"]

1.5 [⅝"]

2.5 [1"]

2 [¾"]

0.5 [¼"]   blindstitch

6. Trim the batting close to the stitching and turn right side out. Blindstitch the opening. Machine quilt.

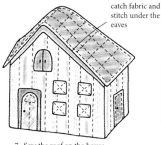

catch fabric and stitch under the eaves

7. Sew the roof on the house.

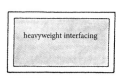

heavyweight interfacing

8. Fuse the heavyweight interfacing on the wrong side of the bottom.

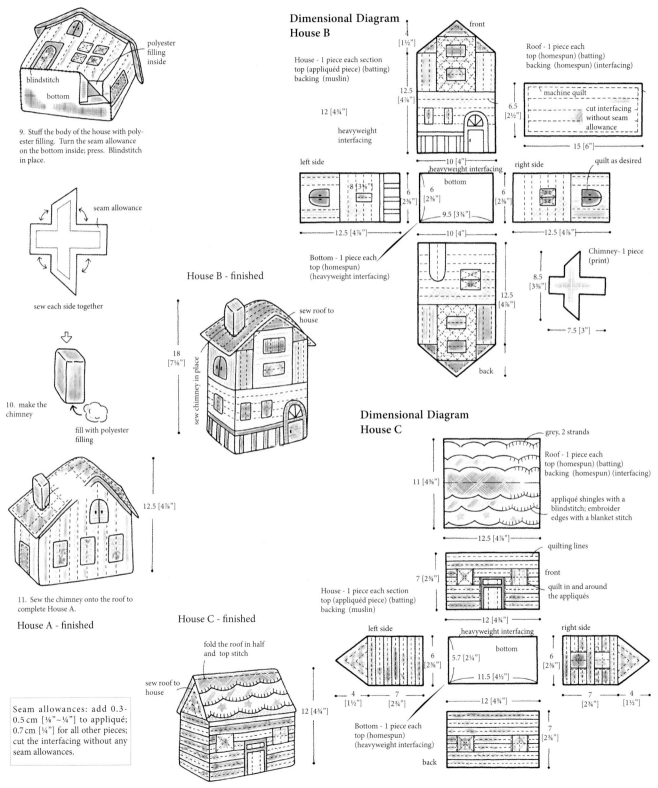

9. Stuff the body of the house with polyester filling. Turn the seam allowance on the bottom inside; press. Blindstitch in place.

polyester filling inside

blindstitch

bottom

seam allowance

sew each side together

10. make the chimney

fill with polyester filling

11. Sew the chimney onto the roof to complete House A.

House A - finished

House B - finished

sew roof to house

sew chimney in place

18 [7⅛"]

12.5 [4⅞"]

House C - finished

fold the roof in half and top stitch

sew roof to house

12 [4¾"]

Seam allowances: add 0.3-0.5 cm [⅛"~¼"] to appliqué; 0.7 cm [¼"] for all other pieces; cut the interfacing without any seam allowances.

Dimensional Diagram House B

front

House - 1 piece each section
top (appliquéd piece) (batting)
backing (muslin)

4 [1½"]

12.5 [4⅞"]

12 [4¾"]

heavyweight interfacing

Roof - 1 piece each
top (homespun) (batting)
backing (homespun) (interfacing)

machine quilt

cut interfacing without seam allowance

6.5 [2½"]

15 [6"]

left side

heavyweight interfacing

8 [3⅛"]

6 [2⅜"]

12.5 [4⅞"]

bottom

9.5 [3¾"]

6 [2⅜"]

10 [4"]

right side

quilt as desired

6 [2⅜"]

12.5 [4⅞"]

Bottom - 1 piece each
top (homespun)
(heavyweight interfacing)

Chimney- 1 piece (print)

8.5 [3⅜"]

7.5 [3"]

12.5 [4⅞"]

back

Dimensional Diagram House C

grey, 2 strands

Roof - 1 piece each
top (homespun) (batting)
backing (homespun) (interfacing)

appliqué shingles with a blindstitch; embroider edges with a blanket stitch

11 [4⅜"]

12.5 [4⅞"]

quilting lines

7 [2¾"]

front

quilt in and around the appliqués

House - 1 piece each section
top (appliquéd piece) (batting)
backing (muslin)

12 [4¾"]

left side

heavyweight interfacing

6 [2⅜"]

5.7 [2¼"]

bottom

11.5 [4½"]

right side

6 [2⅜"]

4 [1½"]

7 [2¾"]

12 [4¾"]

7 [2¾"]

4 [1½"]

Bottom - 1 piece each
top (homespun)
(heavyweight interfacing)

7 [2¾"]

back

Catch-All: **An Old Castle** Shown on p. 36

- The full-size template/pattern can be found on Side C of the pattern sheet inserts.
- Finished measurement: 19 cm [7½"] (w); 15 cm [6"] (h)

Materials Needed

Cottons

- 22 assorted fat quarters or scraps (appliqué)
- Print - 30 × 35 cm [11¾" × 13¾"] (top)
- Dk print - 25 × 15 cm [9⅞" × 6"] (bottom)
- Print - 65 × 50 cm [25⅝" × 19¾"] (backing, partition)
- Print - 20 × 10 cm [7⅞" × 4"] (handle loops)
- Homespun - 2.5 × 60 cm [1" × 23⅝"] (bias binding)
- Muslin - 60 × 35 cm [23¾" × 13¾"] (facing)
- Batting - 60 × 50 cm [23⅝" × 19¾"]
- Fusible interfacing - 60 × 50 cm [23⅝" × 19¾"]
- Flannel - 10 × 10 cm [4" × 4"]
- Waxed cord - 0.3 × 55 cm [⅛" × 21⅝"] (for piping cord)
- Metal O rings - size depends on handle size
- 1 wooden handle
- Embroidery thread - black, red, yellow, brown

Seam allowances: add 0.3-0.5 cm [⅛"~¼"] to appliqué; 0.7 cm [¼"] for piecing and backing; 3 cm [1¼"] for batting and facing. Cut the interfacing without any seam allowance.

Instructions

1. Referring to the full-size patterns and dimensional diagram, cut out all of the pieces of fabric, and batting for the catch-all, as well as the appliqué pieces, adding specified seam allowances.
2. Add appliqué and embroidery to the front and back of the catch-all top; layer the facing and top with the batting in between; baste. Quilt as desired.
3. With right sides together, place the front and back quilted pieces together and sew the sides. Press the seams open.
4. To make the outer bottom, fuse the interfacing to the facing; layer it and the top with batting in between. Baste and then machine quilt.
5. With right sides together, take the front/back catch-all and the outer bottom and pin in place, matching the center and sides; sew them together. Turn right side out.
6. Make the inner bottom by fusing interfacing to the wrong side of the backing. Sew a running stitch around the bottom piece in the seam allowance. Gently pull up the thread to pull the seam allowance in evenly to the edge of the interfacing. Tie off to secure and press the seam allowance to create a perfect oval (see p. 88).
7. To make the lining, fuse interfacing to the wrong side of the backing fabric and sew the side seam to create the inner bag lining. Turn seam allowances under on top and bottom; press. With wrong sides out, sew the inner bottom to the backing using an overcast stitch (diagram 1).
8. Make the pocket partition. Insert and center it in the lining. Using a curved upholstery needle, stitch the partition to the sides and bottom of the lining (diagram 2).
9. Place the lining inside the outer catch-all and align the partition with the outer side seams. Turn the outer catch-all seam allowance under and with opening edges matching, blindstitch the outer quilted piece to the lining along the edge. Leave 4 cm [1½"] on each side seam (centered) to slip in the handle loops
10. Make the handle loops; insert into openings from step 9 and stitch to secure (diagram 3).
11. Make the piping cord from the bias binding and waxed cord (diagram 4) and blindstitch it on both sides to the opening edge. Attach the handle with the metal O rings.

Dimensional Diagram

Front top - 1 piece each
top fabric (appliquéd piece) (batting)
facing (muslin)

Back top - 1 piece each
top fabric (appliquéd piece) (batting)
facing (muslin)

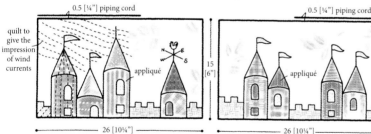

quilt to give the impression of wind currents

0.5 [¼"] piping cord

appliqué

15 [6"]

26 [10¼"]

0.5 [¼"] piping cord

appliqué

26 [10¼"]

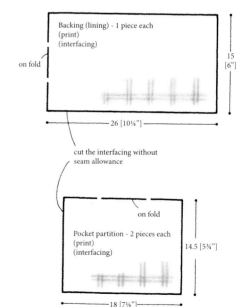

Backing (lining) - 1 piece each
(print)
(interfacing)

on fold

15 [6"]

26 [10¼"]

cut the interfacing without seam allowance

on fold

Pocket partition - 2 pieces each
(print)
(interfacing)

14.5 [5¾"]

18 [7⅛"]

Bottom - 1 piece each
top fabric (dk print) (batting) (interfacing)
facing (muslin)
backing (print) (interfacing)

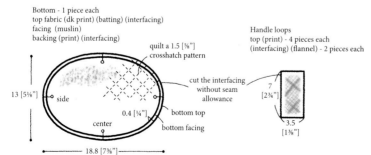

quilt a 1.5 [⅝"] crosshatch pattern

13 [5⅛"]

side

0.4 [¼"]

center

bottom top

bottom facing

18.8 [7⅜"]

Handle loops
top (print) - 4 pieces each
(interfacing) (flannel) - 2 pieces each

cut the interfacing without seam allowance

7 [2¾"]

3.5 [1⅜"]

Diagram 1 - Making the Lining

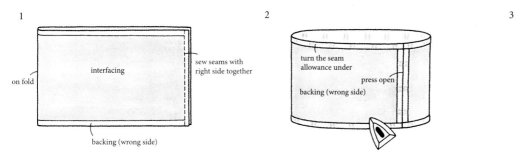

1

on fold

interfacing

backing (wrong side)

sew seams with right side together

2

turn the seam allowance under

press open

backing (wrong side)

3

inner bottom (wrong side)

overcast stitch

backing (wrong side)

Diagram 2 - Making the Pocket Partition

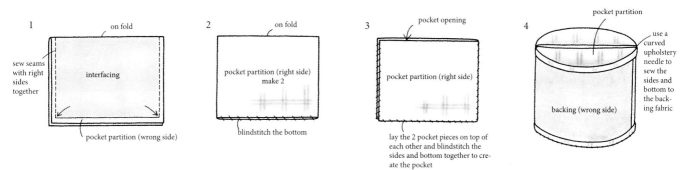

1

on fold

sew seams with right sides together

interfacing

pocket partition (wrong side)

2

on fold

pocket partition (right side) make 2

blindstitch the bottom

3

pocket opening

pocket partition (right side)

lay the 2 pocket pieces on top of each other and blindstitch the sides and bottom together to create the pocket

4

pocket partition

backing (wrong side)

use a curved upholstery needle to sew the sides and bottom to the backing fabric

Diagram 3 - Making and Attaching the Handle Loops

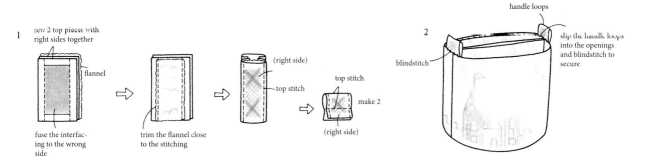

1

sew 2 top pieces with right sides together

flannel

fuse the interfacing to the wrong side

trim the flannel close to the stitching

(right side)

top stitch

top stitch

make 2

(right side)

2

handle loops

blindstitch

slip the handle loops into the openings and blindstitch to secure

Diagram 4 - Making the Piping Cord

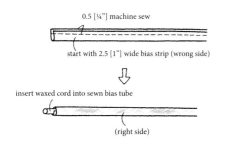

0.5 [¼"] machine sew

start with 2.5 [1"] wide bias strip (wrong side)

insert waxed cord into sewn bias tube

(right side)

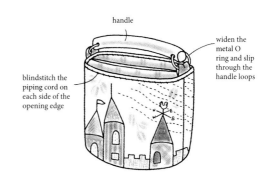

handle

blindstitch the piping cord on each side of the opening edge

widen the metal O ring and slip through the handle loops

Tissue Holder: **Buildings**   Shown on p. 37

- The full-size template/pattern can be found on Side C of the pattern sheet inserts.
- Finished measurement: 12.5 cm [4⅞"] (w) × 13 cm [5⅛"] (h)

Materials Needed
Cottons
- 44 assorted fat quarters or scraps (piecing, appliqué)
- Lt Print- 45 × 30 cm [17⅝" × 11¾"] (top)
- Print- 60 × 45 cm [23⅝" × 17⅝"] (backing, bottom, base sides)
- Print - 15 × 15 cm [6" × 6"] (bottom top)
- Homespun- 3.5 × 60 cm [1⅜" × 23⅝"] (bias binding - upper)
- Print- 2.5 × 60 cm [1" × 23⅝"] (bias binding - inner bottom)
- Homespun- 3.5 × 60 cm [1⅜" × 23⅝"] (bias binding - outer bottom)
- Batting - 50 × 40 cm [19⅝" × 15¾"]
- Fusible interfacing - 40 × 30 cm [15¾" × 11¾"]
- Embroidery thread - dk grey, lt brown, dk khaki, brown, dk brown

Instructions
1. Referring to the full-size template/pattern and the dimensional diagram, cut out pattern pieces and appliqués, adding specified seam allowances.
2. Piece each of the 4 sides and add building appliqués and embroidery.
3. For each of the 4 pieces, lay the top and backing with right sides together and put them on top of the batting, matching edges. Sew both side seams, leaving the top and bottom open. Trim batting close to stitching; turn right side out and press. Quilt as desired. With right sides out, overcast stitch the 4 sides of the tissue holder together to create an open box shape (diagram 1).
4. Make the upper section of the tissue case (diagram 2).
5. With right sides out, place the upper section on top of the box and sew the 4 sides with a sewing machine. Trim the seam allowance to 0.7 cm [¼"] and bind the raw edges with the upper binding. Make a 2.5 [1"] bias binding to bind the inner bottom (diagram 3).
6. Refer to diagram 4 to make the base section for the tissue holder. Measure from one inner side of the box to the other. Use these measurements plus 1.5 cm [⅝"] seam allowance for each side to cut the bottom pieces (top, backing, interfacing, batting).
7. Make the 4 sides for the base section (diagram 5) and attach them to the bottom of the base section. Use the outer bottom binding to bind the raw edges (diagram 6).

Dimensional Diagram

Upper section- 1 piece each
top (lt print) (batting)
backing (print) (interfacing)

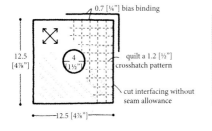

0.7 [¼"] bias binding

12.5 [4⅞"]

quilt a 1.2 [½"] crosshatch pattern

cut interfacing without seam allowance

12.5 [4⅞"]

Seam allowances: add 0.3-0.5 cm [⅛"~¼"] to appliqué; 0.7 cm [¼"] for piecing; 3 cm [1¼"] for batting and backing. Cut the interfacing without any seam allowance.

Sides (4) - 1 piece each side
top (appliquéd) (batting)
backing (print)

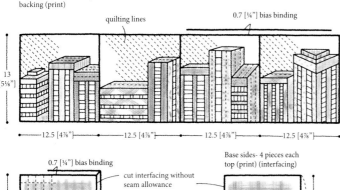

quilting lines

0.7 [¼"] bias binding

13 [5⅛"]

12.5 [4⅞"]   12.5 [4⅞"]   12.5 [4⅞"]   12.5 [4⅞"]

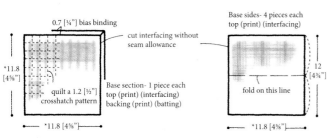

0.7 [¼"] bias binding

cut interfacing without seam allowance

*11.8 [4⅝"]

quilt a 1.2 [½"] crosshatch pattern

Base section- 1 piece each
top (print) (interfacing)
backing (print) (batting)

*11.8 [4⅝"]

Base sides- 4 pieces each
top (print) (interfacing)

12 [4¾"]

fold on this line

*11.8 [4⅝"]

* determine these measurements and cut base section fabric
after determining the actual inner measurements (see step 6)

Diagram 1 - Making the Sides

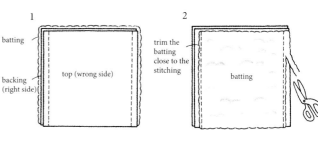

1

batting

backing (right side)

top (wrong side)

2

trim the batting close to the stitching

batting

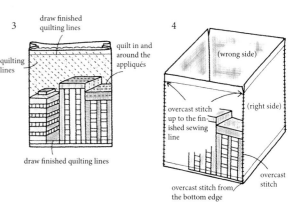

3

draw finished quilting lines

quilting lines

quilt in and around the appliqués

draw finished quilting lines

4

(wrong side)

overcast stitch up to the finished sewing line

(right side)

overcast stitch

overcast stitch from the bottom edge

Diagram 2 - Making the Upper Section

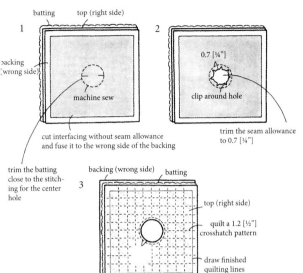

1
batting
top (right side)
backing (wrong side)
machine sew
cut interfacing without seam allowance
and fuse it to the wrong side of the backing
trim the batting close to the stitching for the center hole

2
0.7 [¼"]
clip around hole
trim the seam allowance to 0.7 [¼"]

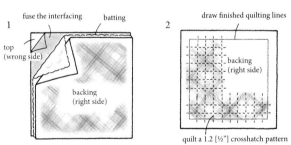

3
backing (wrong side)
batting
top (right side)
quilt a 1.2 [½"] crosshatch pattern
draw finished quilting lines

Diagram 4 - Making the Base Section

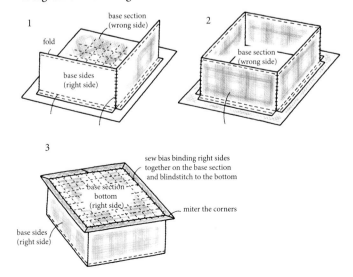

1
fuse the interfacing
batting
top (wrong side)
backing (right side)

2
draw finished quilting lines
backing (right side)
quilt a 1.2 [½"] crosshatch pattern

Diagram 6 - Attaching the Sides to the Base Section

1
base section (wrong side)
fold
base sides (right side)

2
base section (wrong side)

3
sew bias binding right sides together on the base section and blindstitch to the bottom
base section bottom (right side)
miter the corners
base sides (right side)

Diagram 3 - Attaching the Upper Section to the Sides

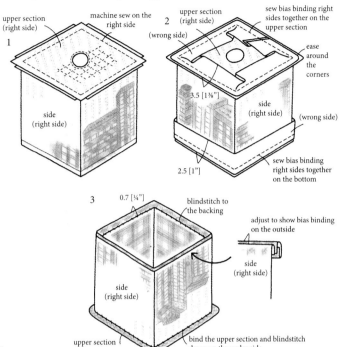

1
upper section (right side)
machine sew on the right side
side (right side)

2
upper section (right side)
upper section (wrong side)
sew bias binding right sides together on the upper section
ease around the corners
3.5 [1⅜"]
side (right side)
(wrong side)
sew bias binding right sides together on the bottom
2.5 [1"]

3
0.7 [¼"]
blindstitch to the backing
adjust to show bias binding on the outside
side (right side)
side (right side)
upper section (right side)
bind the upper section and blindstitch down on the under side

Diagram 5 - Making the Base Section Sides

1
fold
fuse the interfacing
base side (wrong side)
sew the side seams

2
top stitch
base side (right side)
draw finished quilting lines
machine sew on the finished sewing line

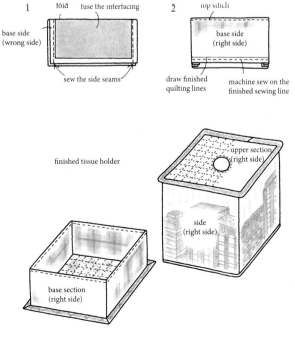

finished tissue holder
upper section (right side)
side (right side)
base section (right side)

Yoko Saito

Quilt Party Co., Ltd.
Active Ichikawa 2-3F
1-23-2, Ichikawa, Ichikawa-shi,
Chiba-Ken, Japan 272-034

http://www.quilt.co.jp (Japanese)
http://shop.quilt.co.jp/en/index.htm (English)

Ms. Saito is a renowned quilter and teacher in Japan who is widely known for her mastery and use of "taupe color". She was introduced to quilting through American antique quilts and has spent over 30 years in the industry. Many of her quilts have been televised on the NHK TV series, "Oshare Kobo" (Fashion Workshop), as well as other TV programs, magazines and books. She serves as an instructor at the NHK Culture Center, Nihon Vogue Gakuen and is the Correspondence Education Division Manager at Nihon Vogue Co. Ltd, as well as being a member of the Japan Needlework Exhibit. She currently owns/ runs a quilt shop and school called "Quilt Party, Ltd.", in Chiba Prefecture, not too far outside of Tokyo.

She has written many books including *American Patchwork, Yoko Saito's Happy Patchwork, Yoko Saito's: Start Quilting with Squares and Triangles* (all published by Quilt Party), as well as *Yoko Saito's Patchwork Learning from the Basics*, and *Just Because I Like Printed Cotton Fabrics* (published by Bunka Publishing Bureau).

Original Title	Saito Yoko no Quilt - House ga Ippai
Author	Yoko Saito
	©2005 Yoko Saito
First Edition	Originally published in Japan in 2005
Published by:	NHK Publishing, Inc.
	41-1 Udagawa-cho, Shibuya-ku,
	Tokyo, Japan 150-8081
	http://www.nhk-book.co.jp
Translation	©2012 Stitch Publications, LLC
English Translation Rights	arranged with Stitch Publications, LLC through
	Tuttle-Mori Agency, Inc.
Published by:	Stitch Publications, LLC
	P.O. Box 16694
	Seattle, WA 98116
	http://www.stitchpublications.com
Printed & Bound	KHL Printing, Singapore
ISBN	978-0-9859746-1-9
PCN	Library of Congress Control Number: 2012948095

Production	Satomi Funamoto (p. 34-35)
	Kazuko Matsumoto (p. 30-31)
	Aiko Yokoyama (p.44)
	Kazuko Yamada
	Yoneko Kusumoto
	Katsumi Mizusawa

Staff

Book Design	Yukiko Inoue (mâne)
Book Layout	Satoshi Tanaka, Yoko Ogasawara (Design House T's) and Yusuke Tsuji
Photography	Miwa Kumon, Masayuki Tsutsui
Editorial Assistants	Chikami Okuda, Naoko Domeki
Stylist	Rieko Ohashi
Illustrations	Michiko Watanuki, Kiyoshi Suzuki
Copyeditor	Hiroko Hirochi
Editors	Maki Okumura, Ayaka Matsubara